KNOWING WHAT YOU SELL

THE KEY TO DOMINATE YOUR MARKET

Lonnie Ayers

Printed in the United States of America

Paperback ISBN: 978-1-736670-4-2
Ebook ISBN 978-1-7366760-3-5

First off, I want to thank my family, especially my wife, Conchita, my daughter Mercedes and son Victor, who spent many years living in the Middle East with me on our long family cultural adventure. I also want to dedicate this book to my brother, Douglas Ayers, who has played sounding board to my many ideas over the years and is my partner-in-crime on our many business ventures.

CONTENTS

Introduction

Do You Really Know What You Sell?

Have you ever been told you could sell ice to an Eskimo? I have. I suspect it is because I grew up selling things, because 1. We were very poor and 2. The answer to every want was to go figure out how to make some money so you could buy it. How poor were we? We didn't have running water for much of my youth nor even an outhouse.

I remember the first time I sold garden seeds as a kid, I think I was about six years old. I had a pretty good springtime run of it; made enough to buy myself a little barbecue. Next year, I learned the value of repeat customers – by not going around to everyone who bought from me last year. I (or rather my mom) started getting calls wanting to know when I would be around as it was planting season.

In the wintertime, aside from all the normal school fund raisers, I also sold personalized Christmas Cards. Thus was the lesson learned about how much people, even fairly poor people, would pay for personalized products. I did a little better at this endeavor, selling those cards for many years.

Then one day, my dad's brother asked about buying an old rusty jeep top we had sitting around, slowly rusting away into the ground. My dad, not yet wise to my ways, said, if you can get him to buy it, for a decent price, you can keep the money. Besides, it is just rusting into the ground. So, I set what I considered a fairly high price, $185 bucks. The next weekend, my mom woke me to show me what that much money looked like. Lesson learned – Always ask for just a bit more. It was a fair price, but not a steal nor a giveaway. But no one expected me to actually get my dad's brother to part with the cash.

My brother and I also set up a mini farmer's market along the highway every year. We sold whatever garden produce was extra, and there was normally a lot. We also found plenty to sell from the woods to the many tourist passing through Brown County, Indiana, from whence I hail. We even managed to sell Fall leaves and rocks, which are in abundance in the area. Lesson learned – Sometimes, you can sell what appear to be worthless things, if you smile and package it right.

Fast forward, after a career in the United States Air Force, and a stint in Saudi Arabia as a contractor and I entered the world of SAP Consulting. Now I was selling software and services. These were contracts with many more zeroes in the price. I remember the first time I pursued and finally closed what was, by SAP standards, a small consulting engagement, only $50,000 for a couple of man-months of work. It took a lot of time and effort, negotiation and finally, a signature in a land where a signed, written contract doesn't actually mean what you think it means. But I got a congratulations from my boss and my paycheck came in on time.

Then, the next contract was for a larger software deal, about $1,500,000 just for the software license. It was about the same amount of work, with demonstrations, business cases, negotiations, and finally, after a cast of what seemed like thousands had reviewed, picked it apart, and otherwise slowed the process down, we had a formal signing ceremony, where we gave the client a golden pen. Then we all had a fancy dinner in an upscale restaurant in Dubai.

Lesson Learned – It takes about the same amount of time and effort to do a 50k deal as it does a $1.5 million deal. But there was another lesson I learned about myself; it was awesome to sign that deal, even if it was making someone else rich. I like to do many things and consider myself to be expert at some of them. But selling, at least when I am successful, I love to do.

Fast forward another 10 years. Now I have no less than 200 SAP deals under my belt, in both a sales role and in a delivery role, as an SAP project manager. Now, I no longer am working alone in a strange land. I am working as the leader of a variety of Virtual Account Teams or VATs for short. The product is so complex, that in order to demonstrate it, it often takes a team composed of anywhere from 3 to 15 Pre-Sales consultants to do the demonstration. A demonstration that, in theory, should only happen after a thorough 'Discovery' process has occurred with the client.

Now we talk about Sales Cycles, often lasting 18 months or more, and on deals where the competition is fierce, with FUD (Fear, Uncertainty and Doubt) being planted by everyone, including the potential customer.

In most cases, and long before this discovery process takes place, I will have received and responded to a complex document known as an RFP or Request For Proposal[1]. If it comes to that, it means we are already behind the eight ball on the deal. Normally, clients will ask us, me in particular, to write their RFP. Or better still, a client will trust me enough to skip the RFP process altogether and just ask me to recommend the best solution based on my knowledge of their business. In short, there's a huge, complex, expensive process that happens before the formal RFP process ever happens.

Now wait a minute, you say, why would a client trust you

---

[1] RFPs are sometimes preceded by RFIs or Request For Interest.

enough to skip an RFP process altogether. Isn't that like letting the fox guard the henhouse?

No, because I know what I am selling.

That's no small statement. Though I no longer work for SAP directly, I have worked for them in various capacities since 1999 and still do SAP Project Delivery work as a Project Manager. In my last internal role with them, I was known as Senior Industry Principle, Value Engineer and Senior Program and Project Manager. In my role as SAP Industry Principal, I was responsible for six Industries in the Middle East, including: Travel & Transportation, Defense, Logistics, Postal, Professional Services, Engineering, Construction & Operations (EC&O) and Utilities. I was a quota carrying Sales Professional, and it was a very significant quota.

Not a Book About SAP

So, what, you say. This book is not about SAP specifically, but I think it is helpful to understand to just what lengths you have to go to know what you sell. It is helpful to know that SAP has an Industry Go-to-Market strategy. This means they have a bunch of different Industry Specific Solutions, about 31 last time I checked. For each of these industries, they have created specialized solutions that are composed of both their core ERP solutions and industry specific solution add-ons that SAP itself produces and many, many partner products.

In order for me to wear that SAP Industry Principal hat and manage those six industry sales pipelines, I had to take SAP Industry Specific Training and Certification, available only to internal people, and then, only to Industry Principals. This training then allowed you to define a Target Solution

Architecture and as well and most critically, define the required software components to be licensed. The complexity here is that most people are trained to think of SAP as modules[2], for instance, Sales and Distribution (SD) or Financial and Controlling (FICO). Industry Solutions, in order to fully support complex industry business processes, require software licenses across multiple modules of SAP. There are a lot of modules.

This is where it is critical to know what you sell. If you sign off on the software license as meeting all the requirements of a client's RFP, and it doesn't, you will end up giving away 'free' licenses to meet their requirement. Me, as an industry principal, needed to know which software license bundles would support an end-to-end business process. In order to do that, I had to understand each client's specific business process and then map that back to the appropriate industry specific software license bundle.

Mistakes here could result in the loss of millions of dollars of revenue and normally, good money going to lawyers to fight it out. It was and is often the case, that I, as a member of the client's Executive Steering Committee[3], would be called on the carpet when someone from SAP didn't get it right.

Not only did I need to know how each of the over 1,300 licensable items on the SAP Software pricing sheet worked, at least at some level, I also needed to know what it would take to implement it. That meant using either internal SAP Consulting teams or external 'partners', who come in all flavors and sizes.

---

[2] There are approximately 16 Core Modules.

[3] Client Steering Committee, Every SAP project, indeed any large dollar project will have an executive committee. These committees are a formal part of the SAP ASAP implementation methodology, have defined roles and specifically, are there to make timely decisions and make sure roadblocks are removed in a timely fashion. They typically control the budget.

The Power of Trust

This is where it really paid to know who you could trust and who was acceptable to the client. Though I hate to say it, price drives everything. Cheaper wins, hands down, every time, unless you know what you're selling and what it is worth to the client. That's why SAP spends big bucks developing tools and methodologies to develop what are called value cases, in plain English, Business Cases

Here, too, it pays to know what you're selling, which, in the case of business cases, is trust. Trust in your numbers, trust in your assumptions, trust in your recommendations. What the reader should know is that clients very much work against you making a solid business case. Sounds terrible and illogical, I know. But think about it, the more solid is your business case, the less of a hammer they have to drive down your price.

Internally, however, they rarely have the expertise to develop their own SAP Specific Business Case. They have the same tools available to them as anyone else when it comes to making ROI calculations. But they do not have the data and business case tools SAP has developed. That's where it starts to make sense as to why they often 'trust' me enough to be on their side of the table.

The honest truth is, this stuff is so complex, that it is impossible to really be biased[4]. All you can really do is really, really study and know the solution you're selling. In my case, that has meant getting SAP Materials Management Certified, SAP Business Warehouse Certified, SAP Strategic Enterprise Management Certified, SAP ASAP Certified, SAP Continuous

---

[4] You often hear the phrase, 'drank the kool-aid' when someone is implying you're 'biased'. What it really indicates is that rather than being biased in a negative connotation kind of way, you're confident in your knowledge about the product.

Business Improvement Certified and SAP Value Engineering certified. In addition, it has meant attendance of a long list of SAP Courses and internal training, such as the SAP Defense Forces & Public Security of DFPS solution. In short, in order to know what I am selling, I have had to invest heavily in training as has SAP.

SAP, the company, has also spent heavily on sending me to a variety of Sales Training courses as well as bringing those sales training courses to me and my teams. I sometimes get to role-play to keep my guys on their toes. It's fun and useful.

Fast forward another 10 years. I am now the proud owner of a small SAP Consultancy, that also happens to be a Hubspot Inbound Marketing and Sales partner. Why Hubspot and why Inbound? Short answer, when I decided to strike out on my own as an SAP Partner, SAP's Middle East Director of Marketing advised me to do more Inbound Marketing, and arranged a demonstration of Hubspot, an Inbound Marketing Platform, which had only been released within the past five years.

Now remember, I am an SAP Project Manager with a considerable sales background. I estimate that between SAP, i2 Technologies and Oracle, I've been responsible, directly and indirectly, for about One Billion USD in software sales over the past twenty years, which I can document. But I did not consider myself a marketer, just good at networking.

In order to build our SAP consultancy, we needed to generate leads, very cheaply. To do that, we went all in on digital marketing. In the process, I took every single Hubspot Certification available, and still retake most of them, every year. At about the 4th year point of our relationship with them as a customer, they reached out and invited us to become partners.

At that point, there were no Hubspot partners that we knew

of, and it was a fairly small, non-publicly traded company. We knew the software as well as any software we have ever used. In fact, I was using it most all day, every day. I had originally thought, when I signed up to be a Hubspot Partner, that my target customer base would be SAP Partners and possibly SAP customers.

We Know What We Sell

Though we have had a fair number of SAP Partners as customers, we have had a far greater number of customers who had nothing to do with being SAP Partners nor SAP Customers. We've had customers in the fashion industry, weight loss industry, accounting and finance, insurance, marketing (yes, other agencies), big data, ecommerce, and many more. How can that be? It turns out it is because we know what we sell, and we know how to sell it.

What we have found with virtually every customer, large or small, is they didn't really know what they were selling. Some were selling a lot, many millions per month, but it became apparent they had gotten lucky when their sales started to drop. They didn't really know what they were selling and thus, their messaging was off, way off.

Others who were in the more higher-value space, such as accounting, had never really had to sell at all. It was all relationship based. The problem was the internet. Much of their work had long ago been wiped out by tools like Quickbooks or sent overseas to be done cheaper. So, like almost everybody else, their strategy had been to move up the value ladder. That ladder is mighty crowded at the top.

Trained On What?

Whereas SAP spent a little money on training an account executive, perhaps giving them an entire week of product overview training, most of the clients we've run across, even if they had the training budget, do not have a formal account executive training curriculum. Why? Because the first step in developing that curriculum is identifying what you sell and what you must know to sell it. This holds true even for low level call center agents, where turnover often exceeds 100%.

I thought you might appreciate a little background about me before you trust me to help you define what you sell.

Summary and Lessons Learned

Though there are many books written about how to sell, few if any have been written about how to figure out what it is you actually sell. I wrote this as a guide for you to think about and ultimately, define and refine your offer:

- **You Need Profound Knowledge** - Most businesses do not have profound knowledge of what they sell
- **Invest Heavily in Your Own Training.** - For complex products, such as SAP, it takes years to truly define what you sell
- **Know the Value of Your Offer.** - Buyers have a vested interest in devaluing your value or business case
- **A Key Resource** - Trust in you counts for far more than you think
- **You Cannot Train What You Cannot Define** - To train your sales force, you must know exactly what you sell
- **Understand the Why** - For your sales force to have the winning edge, they need to understand why buyers buy
- **Make Your Marketing Work Better** - We have found, after years of working with businesses of all sizes, that their marketing suffers because they can't really pin down what the business sells or does.
- **Don't Make This Critical Error** - Many companies cannot clearly define when someone becomes a customer or even what a customer truly is.
- **Learn to Play Well with Partners** - Selling complex products and services often involves many different business partners
- **Follow the Money** - Understanding the financial interest of these business partners is a key task you must master and manage to sell in the big leagues.

CUSTOMERS DON'T KNOW WHAT YOU DO

Your future customer doesn't know or understand what you do. Your future customer probably doesn't really care what you do, either.

Despite what you think you do or sell, every time a new prospective customer knocks on your door, be it a physical or digital door, they must figure out what you're selling. The bigger, more complex your offering, the harder it is for a customer to figure you out. Most fail. Which means you don't make the sale.

Your customer is also jaded. They have often been disappointed by the products or services they have bought. Though your offering may be the best in the world, its reputation is at least partially determined by the actions of your competitors and past experience your customers have had with them.

Your customer is also fearful. Like you, they have limited funds, and a decision to spend those funds on your offering precludes spending that same money on an alternative. If they make a mistake, their job or indeed, their business, is on the line. That's why knowing not only what you sell is critical, helping your future customer see how much more valuable your solution is than a competitors is of paramount importance.

Your customer is also faced with overwhelming complexity. The more features and functions your product has, the more time a customer has to spend figuring out if your offer is what he actually needs. At the consumer level, just to decide on a TV, there are dozens of product parameters to compare and make decisions about. At the business level, especially with large complex systems, it often takes large teams of people to define requirements who then have to spend enormous amounts of time finding solutions. What the business says it needs is written in the language of that particular business. This business specific language is always different from the language you use to describe your offering.

That's why it is critical to know what you sell. It's also why one of your most important tasks is to translate your language into your customer's language. The more customer languages you can master, the more opportunities you will find. It also why if you don't do this translation, it may be because your offering doesn't really fit their need.

The fact that your customers don't know or care about you, are jaded, fearful and mistrustful of you and don't speak your language, is why I wrote this book. It's designed to help you identify what you really sell, how to package and price it, and finally, how to get your customer to know, like and trust your solution, above all others.

CHAPTER ONE

What This Book Is About

This is a book about knowing what you sell. No matter what product or service you sell, if you want to achieve business success, then knowing what you sell and what your customers are buying, is one of the most critical aspects of your business success. It's also one of the most difficult aspects of business, despite what you might think.

Customers Buy Outcomes

Customers, whether they are individuals or businesses, are buying an outcome. Most of the time, this outcome is defined more by them, than by you, the seller. An outcome can be highly specific or very vague. Sometimes, it can be both at the same time.

If you want to achieve success, you'll figure out what the outcome is you want your customer to achieve and orient every aspect of your business around assuring that not only that your customer achieves the outcome they seek, but that you know what that outcome is, in concrete terms, and how it is measured.

Sometimes, your customer will tell you he has a problem, in your language, without really telling you what his true desired outcome really is. This is often because they have not thought about it. For example, what's a plumber's outcome in the eyes of the customer?

If a customer has a leaky pipe, he will call a plumber to get the leaky pipe fixed. But when you ask yourself, why does the customer want to fix the leaky pipe, you realize that he may have many reasons he wants to spend the money on a plumber to get the leaky pipe fixed. Those might include keeping water from damaging the house or running up his water bill. But one level up from this level of analysis, you will see that what the customer really wants is too have clean water continue to come out of his pipes when he turns the faucet on.

Do You Really Know What Your Customers Want?

That's what this book is about - finding out what customers really want and making sure you know what you sell. It's not at all easy. Nor is it simple.

That's why throughout this book I will use 'war stories' and short vignettes to make my point. It is based on the most successful approach to teaching business ever developed, the case study. Consider this a series of case studies all wrapped up in a guide designed to help you uncover what you sell. If you can't currently say what you sell, then this book will help you think through your product or service design. Ultimately, what you sell and what a customer wants, need to perfectly align if you want to dominate your market.

NOT A HOW TO SELL BOOK

This book is about knowing what you sell.

There's already a plethora of books on how to sell out there and this book will not be a recap of those sales methodologies. I will, however, incorporate some of the elements of Consultative Selling into this book in order to tell my story and help you get more out of the book.

A Recap of Well Known Sales Methodologies

Here I will provide only a short paragraph about how each of these methodologies works or is supposed to work. In truth, most sales involve elements from one or more of these methodologies and require the practitioner to be quick on their feet and to adapt to the circumstances.

RECAP OF POPULAR SALES METHODOLOGIES

What is a Sales Methodology?

It is a series of planned actions and responses at the top level. Many of them are trade-marked, while others are just common sense. They are based on common principles, and some are actually based on science, while most are not.

Sales Coaching Enablement

Sales methodologies are really a framework that you can use to work your sales. Like all frameworks, they can and should be modified as the situation demands. They serve at least one other very useful purpose: Facilitate sales coaching. It is very hard for a sales coach to mentor someone without some sort of agreed upon frame of reference.

I have included them so that you are aware of them and as well, can see that for just about any product or service category you might imagine, one or more of these sales methodologies might apply. It's also meant to show that there are a lot of different ways to go about selling, and that, for all practical purposes, it's impossible to say which one is exactly the right approach for your business.

SOLUTION SELLING

Solution Selling has been around for decades and has continuously evolved as customers have achieved a greater buyer maturity level. At its heart, Solution Selling is not about the product, but rather about how the product can help solve a customer problem.

There's a great deal of overlap with other methodologies, such as Consultative Selling. But the basic process is to find that customer pain point, and make sure it hurts, then relieve the pain.

CONSULTATIVE SELLING

This was and is one of the most established, useful sales frameworks. The basic premise is you have to help the customer determine what the correct solution is for their problem, then using tools like an ROI calculator, help a customer justify their decision.

This is a 'heavy footprint' sales methodology, used by the likes of IBM and Accenture. But any business selling slightly complex or expensive 'things' can modify and use it effectively. I've seen marble countertop manufacturers effectively use it.

CUSTOMER-CENTRIC SELLING

This methodology focuses on the challenges, goals, and convenience of the customer. It is fundamentally based on establishing and maintaining a warm, close relationship with the customer. It is unsuitable to productized service sales as the foundation of this methodology is about giving the customer what he wants, even if it means modifying what you're offering.

If you dig deeper into this methodology, you will find much of it is about getting 'into your customer's mind' and employs a lot of different persuasion techniques.

THE CHALLENGER SALE

The Challenger Sale is based on extensive field work observing hundreds of Sales People in action. What the authors found was that there are five basic types of Sales People, but only one stood above the rest.

Those five types were:

- Relationship builders
- Hard workers
- Lone wolves
- Reactive problem solvers
- Challengers

Challengers were consistently found to achieve the best results. What's a challenger? It's someone who forces a customer to examine their own assumptions about what they need or want. The challenger presents the customer with unique insight as to how they might make more revenue or cut costs with their product or service

BASELINE SELLING

Based on using Baseball as an analogy, it distills selling down to a simple, 4 Step process for running the four bases. Comes with a set of tools to use for each step of the Baseline Selling solution.

TARGET ACCOUNT SELLING

This methodology, which Siebel[5] practices and which i2 Technologies[6] was expert at, involves knowing all the players, their roles and motivations in a target account. It is labor intensive, however, with today's networking tools, i.e., LinkedIn, it is much more feasible than it was during the time I used it as an i2 Technologies employee in the early 2000s.

I have to say, in two years, I faced SAP in multiple major accounts, and we won against SAP every single time. Even when our solution was somewhat experimental, we simply blew them away. That's to be expected. SAP's team was up against a very senior SAP guy, me, who knew their every sales move and how to counter it. You will want to be better than that if you want to win. One of the major observations I've made about it is that it often meant winning with an inferior product.

---

[5] A software provider now owned by Oracle, another software provider.

[6] Previously a provider of 130+ different software solutions in Supply Chain Management and other related areas. It has been acquired and absorbed by a series of other software providers.

INBOUND SALES

This is the Hubspot Sales Methodology and is closely coupled with the Inbound Marketing Methodology. In a nutshell, it means that marketing and sales work together to attract customers using valuable content. Once sufficiently 'converted', meaning they've consumed enough of the highly targeted content you produce about your product, then sales closes them. In short, customers come to you versus you chasing them.

ECOMMERCE

I list it here as a sales methodology rather than just a technology. Though it is that. Having set up and ran multiple stores on many ecommerce platforms, such as Shopify and Amazon, I can honestly say it requires just as much thought and effort to sell via ecommerce as it does face-to-face. That's why Amazon reportedly has over 1,400 tests going on every single day. In short, the core secret to successful ecommerce is testing.

Of much more importance is to realize that virtually any product or service can be repackaged and sold via ecommerce. This is true at all price points, and with any level of complexity. I will address productizing your service in a subsequent chapter. I believe it is one of the fundamental forces reshaping the landscape, often in unexpected ways.

JOHN COSTIGAN – HOW TO COLD CALL

John Costigan is the author a book Called "What to Say and How to Say It" as well as an award winning Sales Coach. His speciality is teaching sales teams how to cold call, a dreaded, thankless job. Though it is not formally recognized as a Sales Methodology, I include it here as I believe his approach is valuable for those who are still forced to work cold leads.

He was also a customer of mine, and a very successful one at that.

SNAP SELLING

Launched by Jill Konrath in 2012, SNAP stands for:

- **S**imple
- i**N**valuable
- **A**ligned
- **P**riority

As its acronym implies, this method aims to quicken the sales process with the assumption that prospective buyers will generally be busy and distracted.

SPIN SELLING

SPIN stands for four types of questions sellers should ask their prospects:

- Situation. What is the situation for the prospect right now, as it pertains to your solution?
- Problem. More specifically, how does that situation cause a pain point? Where is the situation broken?
- Implication. What are the results of that problem?
- Need-Payoff. What happens when the problem is solved? What would that look like?

These questions help sellers assess their customers' real situation, isolate the core problems that need to be solved, and lay out the consequences of not solving the problems. Then, they are set up to guide buyers into reframing the situation and imagining how the problem could be solved with their solution.

MEDDIC

MEDDIC stands for:

- **M**etrics
- **E**conomic Buyer
- **D**ecision Criteria
- **D**ecision Process
- **I**dentify Pain
- **C**hampion

This methodology is characterized by a highly disciplined, tech-driven and tightly controlled approach to the sales process.

Using metrics and other relevant data, MEDDIC sets quantitative standards for lead qualification and requires the search and nurturing of a "champion" in the prospect organization who will advocate for the seller's brand/solution.

There is considerable overlap between this methodology and TAS or Target Account Selling

NEAT SELLING

N.E.A.T. stands for:

- **N**eed
- **E**conomic Impact
- **A**ccess to Authority
- **T**imeline

Developed by the Harris Consulting Group and Sales Hacker Inc., this methodology was designed to turn BANT (budget, need, access/authority, timing) on its head. Instead of qualifying customers based on the needs of the salesperson (qualifications for purchase), NEAT selling asks the salesperson to qualify how much they can help the prospect. For example, it requires sellers to achieve the following milestones.

1. Identify "core" needs by probing deep into their customers' challenges.
2. Articulate the value or economic benefit of the solution in terms of ROI.
3. Engage contacts who can influence decision makers when direct engagement is not possible.
4. Set a compelling timeline within which a buyer must make a decision.

VALUE-SELLING FRAMEWORK

This methodology focuses on lead qualification and lead value assessment, enabling sellers to close deals faster and engage only leads with significant impact on their portfolio. Value Selling encourages sales professionals to ask the right questions, articulate the value of a product to the customer's business, and demonstrate flexibility in formulating a mutually beneficial solution.

There's also plenty of overlap with the concept of consultative selling.

A KNOW WHAT YOU SELL BOOK

As you can see, there's no end to Sales Methodologies. I have my own Sales Methodology which I will introduce in this book, but which I have a plan to produce a complete book on.

That's why I wanted to make it clear this book is not a Sales Methodology book. Based on experience that spans decades and dozens of industries, and all sizes of businesses, including even the United Nations, who, as it happens, have an ecommerce operation, I want to explain how to determine what you're actually selling.

I'd like to tell you I have a simple formula for doing that. But instead, I want to use 'first principles' to teach you how I have come to do this over the years and across many products and services.

CHAPTER TWO

What You Sell

PRODUCT OR SERVICE

If you were to design a hierarchy of things you sell, at the very top of the tree would be either a product or service. In many cases, you would find that what you're selling is a combination of physical product and service.

PHYSICAL PRODUCT

A physical product comes in an almost infinite variety of forms. Physical products can range from fairly simple things, like a pencil, to highly complex things, like an Airliner. But just within those two example products, the number and types of variations are amazingly complex.

Let's take that most basic and apparently commoditized product, a pencil. At their most basic level, they come in a basic, everyday form used by people all over the planet, from their first day of school, typically (though not always), as a number 2 yellow pencil.

But then, if you dig a little further under the covers, you find that pencils come in a huge variety of shapes, sizes, colors, and most importantly, with specialized purposes, which can convert them from a mostly disposable 5 cent item to something costing much more. For instance, if you're an architect or mechanical engineer, even though most of what you do is doable with a piece of software, and most likely printed out with a printer, there's still plenty of instances where you need to write in a very specific style, dictated and governed by long established standards.[7]

So, while a number 2 yellow pencil may be perceived as a lowly commodity, a Staedlter[8] Technical Drawing Set contains a huge number of highly specialized writing instruments. You may also find as an architect, you will

---

[7] One such type of standard, GD&T, is known as Geometric Dimensioning and Tolerancing.

[8] They are a major Pencil Supplier, especially in Europe.

need other tools, like a compass, rulers and squares, to get your job done. You will also find that within most any other industry where design is a part of the product, other, highly specialized writing instruments are required, for example, metal workers need metal scribes to make lines in metal.

That's an apparently simple example of a thing that appears and is perceived as a commodity yet, upon closer examination, reveals itself to be a part of a much larger universe of things that all have some relationship, but which have highly specialized 'use cases'.

Let's take one more example of something that is slightly more complicated, an airplane. An airplane is far more complex than a pencil. There are an enormous variety of airplanes, which if, categorized into a product hierarchy tree, would, at the very top of the hierarchy, reveal themselves to be of two basic types: Heavier Than Air and Lighter Than Air. Below that would be Fixed Wing and Rotary Wing and Balloons.

Below this level of product hierarchy, you would find that you have Blimps, Passenger and Cargo Airplanes, Military Aircraft and Helicopters. Below that, you then would start to see an enormous variety of aircraft, from gigantic cargo blimps, to weather balloons, to Four Engine Passenger Jets, to Fighter Jets, to Transport Helicopters. As you continued to classify each type of airplane, you would quickly find that there's a huge number of 'things' that fly, even including drones, missiles and bombs.

Almost all of these types of airplanes are actually

designed to perform an ongoing service, versus being consumed during use, except weapons, which typically, but not always, are consumed upon use.

Summary and Lessons Learned

Selling physical products is one of the oldest and most established sales models. But in today's digital environment, many physical products have some element of information technology embedded in them. There are a number of lessons you should take away from our exploration of selling physical products discussed here:

- **Product Differentiation** - Most products, even products widely perceived as commodities, have opportunities for product differentiation
- **Information Substitutes for Product** - Many products have been dematerialized[9] with today's advancing technological landscape
- **Advanced Manufacturing Technologies** - Dematerialization will only accelerate as manufacturing technologies such as 3D printing, increase their capabilities
- **Competition is Fierce** - Few products are immune from cheaper competitors. Even free products face competition
- **Design in Value** - Much of the value in selling physical products lies in the design of the products
- **Complexity Can Be Good** - Complex products also require complex services

---

[9] Dematerialization refers to finding ways to use less and less material to accomplish the same task. For instance, the amount of aluminum in a can of Coca Cola has been drastically reduced over the years through clever engineering and design.

- **Complexity Can Keep Out Competitors** - Complex product providers present powerful barriers to entry for competitors. Simplifiers[10], however, represent an existential threat to complex product providers
- **Follow-Up to Win** - Follow-on services can and should be wrapped into your product offering
- **Profit in the Service Component** - Much of the profit in what you sell is going to come from those services
- **Better Products Drive Demand For Services** - For just about every product[11] you can imagine, there is some sort of service you can add.

---

[10] Richard Koch: Simplify, Piatkus (April 7, 2016)

[11] Even simple food items, say tomato soup, can include recipes, which is a form of value added service.

SERVICE

A service can take many forms, but probably the central defining characteristic of a service is that it is consumed, but immediately replenished and available to be delivered again and again. There are a huge variety of services that people consume, and many products that need services, such as airplanes, to even be sold or usable in the first place. This is also true of many types of software, i.e., ERP software has to be implemented by professionals.

The challenge with many services is getting a customer to even recognize that a service has been delivered. Let's take some examples from our two product examples. Let's start with the lowly pencil. Pencils get dull. The old solution was to sharpen them with a pencil sharpener or even a pocketknife. The new solution is to make them with replaceable lead. In both of these situations, a service has been performed when the pencil is sharpened. One approach sells a pencil sharpener while keeping the price of the pencil low, while the other eliminates the pencil sharpener, but makes the pencil with the replaceable lead more expensive. In effect, it recreates the razor blade model or the printer and ink model.

When it comes to airplanes, there are many, many services that must be consumed in order to make them do what they are designed to do, which is fly people and things from point A to point B. For example, every aircraft requires an extensive series of maintenance actions, which occur over time as well as with specific usage. This means an aircraft can generate a service requirement just sitting there, due to the passage of time. If it is flying, it normally will generate a service requirement based on flight hours. But it may also incur additional maintenance service requirements based on how it was flown during those hours. For instance, a fighter jet, if overstressed, meaning it pulled more G's[12] than it was supposed to, will require extensive, additional maintenance.

But an airplane is a fairly special case when it comes to services. It requires an extensive infrastructure of complex service delivery entities to get people into their seats, cargo in the belly or targets serviced. Someone has to sell tickets, be that a website or travel agent, someone has to work the gates to provide them with their boarding pass, process their luggage and get them on their way. Someone else has to prepare meals, called catering, and get it to the plane, on time, not before and not after. Someone else has to fly the plane and provide services to the passengers during the flight. On top of all these many services, someone else had to develop a destination for the passenger to want to go too.

As you can see, within this complex eco-system, there are many players, and anyone wanting to act as a seller within this complex supply chain, will have to know exactly what he is selling and how it fits within this system of systems. It should also be obvious that most of the players in these scenarios are probably going to be fairly

[12] G's means in this case, force of gravity. 1 g is what is exerted on you just sitting on the couch. 9 G's means you weigh 9 times as much and is what a fighter pilot will experience in a tight turn, right before he passes out. The airplane will also experience the same force during this turning maneuver.

large, meaning it takes a lot of money to set up a business and compete in this arena. Want to work in catering? You're up against a global player called GateGourmet[13] who has billions invested in a global delivery network. But perhaps you can sell them software that makes their business more efficient, which is exactly what we did in one of my previous companies.

The central message here is that a business eco-system can and does have many players. If you want to compete within an established system, in this case, airline passenger transportation, it can be done, but it will require a vast amount of capital. However, there are always smaller, more tactical areas where you might be able to compete if you're a new player trying to penetrate the market. In order to find these opportunities, you will need to really get to know your target market. You'll also need to know exactly what you sell.

---

[13] GateGourmet is mentioned only because the author has some passing experience with them from a previous engagement in the Supply Chain Management space.

Summary and Lessons Learned

Selling services is one of the largest sales activities in existence. In today's digital environment, service design is a key activity of every business that has any element of service in their offering. There are a number of lessons you should take away from our exploration of selling services discussed here:

- **Know Your Outcomes** - Services can be an excellent business model if you know your outcomes, that is, know what outcomes your customer achieves
- **Look For Additional Opportunities** - Many products provide a services add-on sales opportunity
- **Reduce Inventory Cost -** Services mostly eliminate the need for physical inventory, which provides a tremendous advantage
- **Higher Profit Margins Live Here** - Services can yield very high profit margins, if designed and delivered correctly
- **Get Your Pricing Right** - There are many, many services pricing models
- **Sell on Value** - Customers, especially in the IT space, have been conditioned to "by-the-hour" rates[14], which eliminates the possibility to sell on value. That's why you need to be making your business case early in your sales cycle

---

[14] Alan Weiss, Million Dollar Consulting

- **Couple Services And Products** - Many products can only be sold if accompanied by services, often complex services
- **Be Flexible and Win the Day -** Many buyers want to buy those services separately from the product
- **Look for Service Opportunities Everywhere And In Every Time** -There are service opportunities available on products that were sold years ago, or even centuries ago
- **Know Your Service's Value to The Buyer -** The seller who knows what value his service brings to the buyer and can make that case can protect his margins and make his product easier to purchase in the eyes of the buyer

PRODUCTIZED SERVICE

For many sellers, the secret to success is to create a productized service. What is a productized service? Though there are probably many possible definitions, I am defining it as having a defined set of deliverables with clearly defined outcomes and within a specific scope.

That's management consulting speak for defining exactly what you will do and deliver and ideally, to a specific type of audience, which marketers like to refer to as Buyer Persona while sellers refer to them as Ideal Customer Profiles or Ideal Buyers. You'll notice that I freely mix these somewhat ambiguous terms. That's because there isn't a clearly delineated dividing line between the various concepts mentioned.

What are some common examples of Productized Services? As it happens, I've been working on developing my own productized service. As part of that development project, I have run across a variety of productized service offerings. I will just walk you through a few of the more interesting ones I've run across and let you know up front that some of them may have disappeared by the time this book is published. But I believe each of the of the following examples have valuable lessons for those who want to develop their own productized service offering. First, let's take one most of us have seen every day but have never thought of as a productized service – oil changes.

There are many players in this space, including JiffyLube and Wal-Mart. This is a low margin, high volume business that is easily consumed. What can you learn from it? You can turn what was once a grungy, messy job into something almost anyone can have done, often in 20 minutes or less. That's why it's worth just a bit more to have one of the service providers perform this service. It not only is very fast, cheap and convenient, it eliminates you, the end consumer from having to have the physical infrastructure to do an oil change.

Ok, that one was an obvious one. How about one that is a bit more complicated. In this case, writing Customer Testimonials as a service. I've found at least two different service providers who have taken on, very successfully, the task of building a customer testimonial[15], most typically on behalf of software providers.

I think this service, which has a product, i.e., written and or video customer testimonial as a deliverable, is a well thought out, exceptionally targeted, niche, productized service. If you never had to get a customer testimonial, you may not appreciate how tough this is to deliver. Within my industry, SAP ERP, no matter how successful a project implementation may have been, customers are extremely reluctant to give testimonials. Why is it so difficult? Some would argue because the customers aren't happy. The hard reality is, lawyers are usually the culprit. They have, wrongly or rightly, often advised their clients to never give testimonials. This same advice is often why you rarely see a consultant who can get positive referrals from past clients, with a few exceptions of

---

[15] Meg Cumby, https://megcumby.com/

course. To overcome this issue, SAP employs an army of internal people who are assigned this task. It must work, SAP has literally thousands of customer testimonials from every industry segment and for every solution they offer.

Why are these testimonials so important, and yet given so parsimoniously? Because, frankly speaking, most SAP projects are 'significant emotional events' and involve a lot of change within the client organization. Beyond that, most IT managers simply don't want to help a service provider. There's a lot of reasons for this, including that the service provider will have more 'leverage' on any subsequent service project within that customer. Yet other customers actually try to get you to sign contracts that prohibit any positive references being given nor will they accept any customer reference visits.

That's why a productized service offering to get these customer testimonials, if it works, and it seems to work, is a very useful service, worth a lot of money to any SAP partner and SAP itself.

That's an example of a productized service offering that is extremely niched down. But what about if your product is more complex, for example, you implement entire systems as a productized service offering.

One common example I've run across is installing the hardware during an SAP implementation. These are projects that often run six months or more. Yet, there is a well defined sequence of events that define this productized service offering. The unique characteristic of this example is that the productized service actually requires multiple service providers, in this case, SAP and one or more hardware and network infrastructure vendors.

It all starts with an initial 'scoping' using an SAP tool called [16], which kicks off a second tool, which consist of a series of detailed questionnaires from the hardware vendor. After all the sizing is completed, a completed, detailed Bill of Materials is produced, using a series of internal software tools, that then become part of the hardware order.

After that, there is an installation project, which is highly defined, even when it involves constructing new facilities. Sounds very complicated, but keep in mind, this happens between 8000 and 9000 times a year, so there has been plenty of time and experience to refine it down to this highly orchestrated process.

How do you productize something so complicated as a giant IBM server installation or something as seemingly simple as writing a Case Study? At a high level, it helps to have delivered it before. But what if you have never done it before? Here's where it helps to be a project manager, as I happen to be.

Though I have access to and always use my own copy of Microsoft Project[17], I realize most people don't have $1,500 or more bucks to drop on the program. You can always use Excel or if on a Mac, Numbers, to get most of the following done, however, the reader should understand that using only Excel

---

[16] Quicksizer*

[17] Microsoft Project is a Software Product Designed to Manage Projects

to plan out a service has quite a few not so obvious risks.

Productizing a Service Step-by-Step

Assuming you have a project planning tool, here's how you do it:

- You make a list of the deliverables.
- You create a Work Break Down Structure (WBS)[18] in your tool (this can be more or less automatically generated in MS Project) but I generally develop a specific one for my projects. You should also be aware that WBS structures are often pre-defined by clients like the US government.
- For each individual deliverable, estimate how long it will take to deliver it as a final product.
- Create a Resource Sheet[19] in MS Project. Assign a cost per hour to the resource.
- Assign a resource to each deliverable
- Assign dependencies between tasks. This is not easily done in Excel or Numbers
- Run a Project Cost report within the tool. You now have the basics of what your productized service

---

[18] A Work Break Down Structure or WBS is a way to graphically represent the deliverables of a project. They can follow a highly specified naming convention, or the default provided by MS Project.

[19] A Resource can be a Person or Thing or a combination of the two. For example, a coder can cost so much an hour but also require the use of an associated tool, which also has a cost associated with it, and both can be assigned to a task and the system will calculate the cost to deliver it.

will consist of and how much it will cost to deliver it

- Now, to price your productized service. Add in your overhead and target profit.
- Put up your pricing page and include the list of deliverables. Provide a way for your client to pay i.e. a payment button.

That's how I, a Senior SAP Project Manager, actually deliver every SAP project (except for the markup, which has usually already been added into the SOW or Statement of Work).

This entire process can be done in under 30 minutes if you're familiar with the tool. I've done this many times for clients. That's why if you have access to an example project plan, this process goes much faster. It's also why many professional service organizations keep a copy of them from every project.

The challenge, of course, is defining exactly what you will deliver and estimating how long it will take. That's where the continuous improvement cycle kicks in. As you deliver each new project, you will need to update your Standard Operating Procedures or SOPs. In essence, you will be developing an engineered time standard.

There are many, many other examples of productized services, and you can find a complete list in the Appendix A.

They broadly fall into these categories:

- Marketing and SEO (Search Engine Optimization)
- Podcasting
- Content Writing
- Graphic Design
- Wordpress Maintenance
- Reporting and Analytics
- Finance & Legal Services
- Coaching
- Support
- Travel
- Health

Summary and Lessons Learned

Selling productized services is one of the fastest growing approaches to sales in existence. In today's digital environment, designing your productized service is a key activity of every business that has any element of service in their offering. There are a number of lessons you should take away from our exploration of designing and selling productized services discussed here:

- **Clients Know Exactly What To Expect** - Your pricing page lays out the exact scope of what you will deliver
- **You Now Sell Outcomes** - Though your project plan is a deliverables oriented, WBS organized set of deliverables, the client is interested only in outcomes. You can now incorporate this concept into your offering.
- **You No Longer Spend Time Writing Custom Proposals** – Your pricing page is your proposal and they accept it by pressing the buy button
- **You Can Launch Your Productized Service In A Day** - Tools such as Clickfunnels[20] come with everything you need to get set up using a template with a payment gateway. You just hit your email list to get started

---

[20] Clickfunnels is a type of software that allows you to set up marketing and sales funnels. It comes with many templates from a variety of industries to help you get your funnel set up faster.

- **Far Easier To Sell** – You have a defined set of deliverables which is clear to the customer. If they want more, that will cost more, conversely, if they want a lower price, you offer less service
- **You Eliminate the Danger of Non-Payment** - By getting paid upfront, there is no risk of a customer not paying.
- **Increase Your Income** – Your system is scalable and not dependent upon how many proposals you pitch nor how many hours you work during the day
- **Engineered and Automated Service Delivery** – Using Standard Operating Procedures (SOPs), you can now concentrate on outsourcing each part and on improving your SOPs with each new customer
- **Improve Your Marketing Results** – By productizing your service, you will have a more highly refined target market to target. That makes targeting your messaging far easier using SEO
- **You're Building a Sellable Asset**[21] – By building a standardized service, you can now sell it as it is highly attractive to investors as a money making machine

---

[21] In reality, a productized service is very similar to a franchise. Franchises have typically already defined in minute detail what a franchisee is supposed to do and deliver.

CHAPTER THREE
Uncover The Need

DECIDING WHAT TO SELL

It is often the case that you're already in business; perhaps you inherited one from your family. In those cases, you don't have much to decide. Somebody made the decision for you. But perhaps you're like one of the nearly 350,000 to 420,000 people who are starting a new business each month*[22] in the USA, which, by the way, is up from 250,000 a month, the average during the Obama Administration.

That's a lot of new businesses. Most are probably in what are very mundane, yet potentially lucrative areas, such as restaurants, plumbers and florist. Others may well be in what will become Unicorn businesses, such as networking, that may become Billion Dollar plus businesses. Perhaps you're part of a partnership which brings substantial money to the table, and will be building out something that requires much more capital, such as a new car company.

I think it is actually very inspiring that so many people are starting businesses, despite the odds being stacked heavily against them. As the saying goes, hope springs eternal.

If you want to be one of the select few who manage to start a business and succeed, at least past 5 years, what should you do?

[22] New Business Formations, https://www.census.gov/econ/bfs

MARKET RESEARCH

Given the availability of so much information today, it is far more feasible to conduct market research than it has ever been. Nevertheless, it is still a good idea to conduct both quantitative and qualitative market research using the available data that you can find on the internet as well as the public library.

Regardless of whether you intend to build a business and take it public or simply want to build a business that supports a certain lifestyle, one of the key data points you will want to focus on is the Total Addressable Market or TAM for short. There is fairly accessible information on a vast array of business types when it comes to TAM for virtually any market segment.

For instance, I've got a client who specializes in SAP Warranty Management software implementation. Though any single SAP Warranty Project is probably in the 2 to 3 million dollar range, if you research the TAM for Warranty Management Software, you'll find that the annual Total Addressable Market is estimated to reach $3.4 Billion USD by 2020. Though that sounds like a lot, that's for all types of warranty management software.

Now you have to decide on whether or not it is an attractive enough market for you to target. Here's where it helps to know a bit about a market, in this case, the market for ERP software. As it happens, I know a lot about the overall market share of Commercial Off-the-Shelf (COTS) ERP software versus legacy system software.

In particular, I know that only about 20% of all businesses who could use an ERP system have opted for a commercial system. Of the available commercial ERP systems, SAP is by far the leading vendor, with about a 60% market share, while Oracle is a close second, followed by Microsoft. But then there are about 50 other ERP vendors in the market space.

SAP has stated publicly[23] that they acquire between 8000 and 9000 new customers per year, and that their sales roughly match the shape of the U.S. business landscape. That shape is a triangle, with a few very large businesses at the top, known variously as the Fortune 500 or Fortune 1000, and thousands of Mid-Size Companies in the middle of the pyramid. Below that, are millions of small businesses, often consisting of one person, the owner.

For my client, it is very apparent that his product is not a mass market appeal product. In fact, within the overall warranty software management space, SAP holds a minuscule market share of .05%[24] which works out to be +~$170,000,000 per year available to be captured.

Nevertheless, a few projects won can and have made him a millionaire. But can he grow to the next level without expanding his target offering? Not easily, as he has neither a monopoly position nor a unique add-on product to insert into the mix.

---

[23] SAP Investor Relations https://www.sap.com/docs/download/investors/2020/sap-factsheet-jan2020-en.pdf

{$NOTE_LABEL} https://www.marketsandmarkets.com/Market-Reports/warranty-management-system-market-121693448.html

The point of all this market research is that you can definitely get a leg up on the competition if you target a market which is large enough. However, the larger the addressable market, the more competition you're likely to encounter.

Summary and Lessons Learned

Conducing market research remains a key activity in determining what to sell. In today's digital environment, there is more information than ever to exploit to uncover your true market. There are a number of lessons you should take away from our discussion on conducting market research:

- **Ensure Your Ocean is Large Enough -** Your target market needs to be large enough for you to address
- **TAM -** The TAM or Total Addressable Market is the annual value of the market
- **Use Google Search -** The availability of TAM information is often times easily found by conducting a simple Google Search
- **You Get What You Pay For -** But free information should not be fully trusted. Instead, try to source information from various providers
- **Vary Approach by Product Type -** There are major differences in doing market research for a completely new product versus an established type of business
- **Customer Segmentation -** Market research is key to successfully developing granular customer segmentation data
- **Many Methodologies -** There are a huge variety of market research methodologies
- **Good Guess -** All market research ultimately yields

a good guess as to who your potential customers actually are

- **Know Your SIC Code -** Sometimes, the US Government SIC[25] codes are useful places to start your research, sometimes not. Always bear in mind that these codes and their meaning change over time and companies self-identify their SIC codes
- **Invest Enough in Research -** Be prepared to spend 'substantial' dollars on good market research

---

[25] SIC Codes, Standard Industry Classification codes, https://www.sec.gov/info/edgar/siccodes.htm

COMPETITOR RESEARCH

You Can Do This

You don't need an MBA to know you need to conduct competitor research. But it definitely helps to know about a few of the tools MBAs use to conduct competitor research and to formulate strategies to defeat their competition.

Competitor research is a multi-step process that should be a regular part of your on-going strategic planning, even if you're a one-man army.

Identify Your Competition

The first step is to identify who your competitors are. That presupposes you already know exactly what you sell.

Sometimes, it is obvious who is competing with whom. McDonalds vs. Burger King, Ford vs. Chevy, Lowes vs. Home Depot, Boeing vs. Airbus.

Other times, it may not be so obvious to the general public. A Drilled Water Well vs. Cistern vs. City Water. DIY (Do it Yourself) vs. Done For You. ICE (Internal Combustion Engine) vs Electric. Inbound Marketing vs Outbound Marketing. Written Word vs. Video.

The list could go on and on. You may notice that some of these match ups are not so obvious competitors. If you were to ask some of them, providing they would talk to you, they would deny they are even competing. For instance, Lowes vs. Home Depot have positioned themselves in the market as being mostly for contractors vs. Do It Yourself (DIY) home owners doing a small project. Yet both have evolved to sell a bit of what the other is selling, including providing education to drive sales.

Some competition is much more nuanced. For instance, the competition between using the written word, i.e., blogs to drive lead generation vs. using video is highly nuanced. There's already an established field of players who will write for so much a word. Within this universe of writers, there is a vast range of quality, which means pricing and results vary greatly.

There's also a whole universe of service providers who produce video in all its many forms. If you're a business owner, trying to decide which of these two approaches is the best to take to generate leads for your business, you will find it very hard to decide until you spend money to have it done so you can measure results.

But if you're a video producer, you will find you're torn between wanting to be a storyteller versus a lead generation machine. Both tasks require different skills, take a lot of time and effort and can cost a lot of money. There's no shortage of video content out there. How do you compete in that market space?

Analysis Step

Once you've identified your competitors, the next step is the analysis step, normally using a tool called SWOT analysis, or Strengths, Weaknesses, Opportunities and Threats. Conducting a SWOT analysis can be time consuming as one must be done for each competitor. The more competitors you identify, the more time you have to invest in this analysis exercise.

The other challenge with conducting a competitor SWOT analysis is that you have to make a lot of assumptions based on publicly available information, which may not consist of much. These assumptions mean there is some degree of uncertainty contained within any SWOT analysis. There is also the ever-present danger of underestimating a competitor's strength because you over estimate your own strength.

There are at least two other common types of analytics tools you can use in your competitive analysis[26].

- 4 Quadrant Competitive Landscape Chart
- Mindmap

The 4 Quadrant Competitive Landscape Chart is a way to organize your competitors into different buckets. You slot a competitor into each Quadrant, whose meaning or value you define. Their meaning is usually specific to your situation versus theirs. For example, perhaps they are identified as Low Cost, High Cost, Easy Availability, Hard Availability

Mindmaps, one of this author's favorite tools, can be used in many situations, and as they are 'your' minds' map of how things work, they are unique to each person who

---

{$NOTE_LABEL}
https://www.google.com/search?q=4+quadrant+charts+of+the+competitive+landscapes&client=firefox-b-d&tbm=isch&source=iu&ictx=1&fir=-3ggbLtTyeCopM%252CbKruu39ag4F_yM%252C_&vet=1&usg=AI4_-kSeceKhKqywR9SObLxCcUDNWoa-Dg&sa=X&ved=2ahUKEwiAoLn_wtLtAhXhmFwKHQ65BVMQ9QF6BAgMEAE#imgrc=qypwYcjrMGwizM

produces one. When it comes to using them for competitive analysis, they are great as they allow you to go 'freestyle' with your analysis. You can also use them to develop a plan to match, block or exceed a competitor.

Decide Where You Will Play

If, after having conducted all the previous steps, you still decide to pursue your business idea, now you really have to refine your offer. The whole point of conducting all this time-consuming competitor research is to help you validate your idea or strategy, then decide what you will sell.

It may be that you're already running a business. In that case, this research should inform your product development[27] decisions going forward. This may sound like some wonky headed MBA talk, but almost any business of any size needs to do this.

Some of my clients, who may already be quite successful, have decided, after asking me to look at their marketing numbers, to come up with completely new offers. It is almost always the case that a previously high performing offer is suffering from a competitors attack.

Sadly, sometimes the result of a competitor analysis will force you to come the conclusion not to compete. There's nothing wrong with this decision. The trick is to make the decision early, before you've invested too much in your endeavor.

Other times, the conclusion will be that you're not

---

[27] Reinertsen, Donald G.. The Principles of Product Development Flow: Second Generation Lean Product Development . Celeritas Publishing. Kindle Edition.

currently well positioned against your competitors, but that it is a market worth pursuing. In which case, you must develop a new, competitive offering. This happens a lot. Just look at how many consumer goods come to the market each year.

Incorporate Your New Knowledge About Competitors

As I have done in other chapters, I want to give you a couple of real-world examples of how I used competitor research to refine my offering and more specifically, how in one case, I used it to develop my annual business plan.

In my previous role working for the blue team, as a Senior Industry Principal, one of my not so pleasant tasks was preparing my annual industry business plan. Keep in mind, I actually had to prepare six of these, as I 'owned' six different industries, including:

1. Professional Services
2. Engineering, Construction & Operations
3. Aerospace & Defense
4. Postal
5. Logistics
6. Travel & Transportation.

This process was basically a six-week marathon of information gathering, strategizing, and running the numbers. It was also heavily reliant upon a huge competitor analysis mega model (literally, called the mega model) that cost a small fortune. Its value was twofold with regards to annual business planning.

The first was that it gave an estimate of the size of the market, by industry, and specifically solution - relevant to the ERP market. Within our domain, of which ERP was the central core offering but not remotely close to the only offering, this provided invaluable information about the size of the addressable market.

The second was that it gave detailed information on all of the competitors expected to be present in our market. The market was very, very crowded, and still is. It also gave us a rating of each competitors strength, vis-à-vis our offering. When you combined these two competitive dimensions, plus my own knowledge of the market, you had the basis for planning.

But planning without action and more importantly, budget, is useless. That's where the next step in our competitor analysis fueled business planning came into play. That was to drive product development.

Business planning was, of course, designed to drive your annual revenue plan. But it was also designed to allow you to identify 'white space', meaning identifying where market opportunities existed, but for which we did not have an offer. This then, was used to drive software development decisions by the product marketing group.

Like all businesses, the blue team had far more market opportunities than ability to develop a solution. That meant, from my perspective, with bottom line P&L responsibility for my industries within my region, that if I wanted to increase my sales, then I had to have a way to make a stronger business case for additional development or acquisition than any of my fellow Industry Principals.

This meant quantifying the size of the opportunity, assigning probabilities of winning and based on macro and micro level competitor analysis, estimating the ability to win. In the longer term, this process was how you truly understood what you were selling and how much you could expect to make. It was also how you estimated how much budget you would need to pursue these deals.

Tactical Use of Competitor Information

The annual business planning process is just one of the ways competitor analysis is useful. There was another use which was much more tactical in nature, and that was preparing competitor battle cards.

What's a competitor battle card? Well, if the mega model was 'high level' information, a competitive battle card was much more tactical in nature. Not every company, at least small ones, will have a department dedicated to developing these, but you can still do one, even if you're a one-man army.

A competitor battle card comes in two flavors; one contains general data points about a competitor and the other one is a customized battle card about a competitor tailored to a specific opportunity. They help answer two questions and accomplish one big goal.

The two questions are:

1. **Can We Win**
2. **How We Lose**

You can and should use these battle cards in every deal to sow FUD, (Fear, Uncertainty and Doubt) about your competitors. That's why it is very important to quickly find out who you're competing with in any deal. This can be a challenge, as clients oftentimes don't want you to know, for not so obvious reasons. But you can find out; I've often ran across the competitor in the parking lot right before I was about to go in to deliver a demonstration. Situational awareness goes a longways toward accomplishing your goals.

The big goal they help you accomplish is positioning your offering in a more competitively advantageous position against your competitors. When millions of dollars are on the line, this becomes critical. To do this, it is often necessary to use many players on your team to plant this FUD. If you're part of a larger organization, this means arranging "C" level meetings between your side and the prospect's side. It can also mean educating partners on competitive differentiators between your product and known competitors.

Educating partners can serve two purposes. One is to make sure you and your partners are fully aligned and equipped with the latest information, so everyone is better equipped. The other one is less obvious. Just about every partner eventually wants to expand their offering. Meaning, for example, a partner who previously only offered solutions from SAP, may now also start offering solutions from Oracle and Microsoft.

They have to make a decision on every deal then,

whether they want to partner with you or your competitor. That's why it helps to keep educating partners on the competitive weakness of your competitors in a deal. They may well decide to go with you and thus, you've taken one more player off the battlefield. Yes, this is somewhat like playing chess.

Summary and Lessons Learned

Conducing competitor research is a key task every business needs to conduct. There's more competition than ever before, no matter what product or service category you might be targeting. There are a number of lessons you should take away from our discussion on conducting competitor research:

- **Be a Good Researcher -** Use all your resources to conduct competitor research
- **You Need Some Budget -** Don't be afraid to buy a competitor's product or service. You will often learn a lot this way
- **Look Around -** Don't just focus on direct competitors
- **Avoid Being the Blood in the Water -** You can often find 'blue ocean' space among your competitors offerings
- **Go Full Spectrum -** When researching your competitors, look at everything you can find about them, including their prices, discounts, upsells, cross-sells and bundled offers
- **The Dog That Don't Bark -** Look at what your competitors do not offer as well. They may have missed the opportunity you see.

- **Financial Literacy is a Must -** Learn to read a

financial statement - the strength of your competitors can often be found in those financial statements. Avoid attacking their strength, instead, look for weakness.

- **It Can Be Expensive to Take Out a Competitor -** Decide whether you will go head-to-head against a competitor or avoid them
- **A Safe Alternative - But Not Good For You -** For many sales, your biggest competitor is 'do nothing'
- **Staring You in the Face -** Can you uncover your competitor's priorities from their public statements about priorities?

PARTNERING

Partner for Success

As you climb up the value ladder, you often find that what you sell is not enough to meet the full spectrum of what your customer is asking for. What that means is you often need to partner up to be able to bid on a project.

In my role as SAP Industry Principal, I often had to put together a consortium of partners in order to bid on an RFP[28]. Why would SAP, a hundred-billion-dollar company, need to partner? It's hard to explain, but I think a couple of case studies from real world partner consortiums I had to put together will help to explain it.

The first was for a series of new airports the government of Oman was going to build, if memory serves, 5 of them in total. SAP is not in the construction business, but the RFP came to us for a bunch of different reasons, including past networking activities by me and various members of the extended team, both SAP and partners. The problem was, the RFP was for all of the airport IT systems and much more.

An airport has many systems, of which an ERP system is only a part. A much bigger system is the AODB or Airport Operating Database. When I had finished analyzing the RFP, the only option I had was to not only reach out to my known SAP partners but as well to partners that SAP had no relationship with.

---

[28] Request for Proposal, a document issued by a buyer looking for suppliers to meet a need the buyer has. Often highly complex, and very often, incomplete.

That ultimately translated into me traveling around the Middle East, Europe and other points to meet and greet communications systems providers, electrical system providers and many others.

Strategically, we made the decision to step back from taking the lead and instead assembled not one, but nine different consortiums with different capabilities and probabilities to win. That's what it takes when you have opportunities that are beyond the scope of your offering and yet well worth winning. We did ultimately win it.

If that is an example of a complicated, if unusually complex partnering arrangement, a more typical arrangement is when we would have to put together a consortium of known SAP partners with specific delivery capabilities.

For instance, SAP doesn't sell hardware, so we virtually always had to bring in a hardware partner, as SAP usually requires 'big iron[29]' and then some. Other SAP Partners typically required include implementation partners, networking partners, change management partners, training partners, and many others. In the most extreme example, a Greenfield[30] SAP implementation for a Big Box retailer, I had to deal with 31 different service providers, including cash register experts, payment gateway providers and membership printers, to name just a few.

---

[29] Big Iron refers to very large computers, typically mainframes, that can be expanded as needed. Even these are often not big enough, and Big Iron often grows into Big Data Centers with dozens or hundreds of mainframe class computers. For many large customers, they may have multiple, geographically separated data centers, both owned and leased.

[30] Greenfield refers to a customer with no pre-existing SAP system installed.

That's par for the course for large projects. It's also a challenging environment for the client as they now have to deal with many different people when it comes to 'issues'.

So, what does it take to partner effectively? In my experience, it works best when the parties bring unique, complimentary capabilities to the table. If there is much overlap, for instance, if both partners can deliver SAP consulting, then there will be friction. But if one partner has a solution that fills whitespace that the other does not have, then it can work very well.

Partners Need to Commit to Deal Value

So far, I've only talked about partners you bring into a deal. For large IT and other types of firms, the partners are positioned as both sales and delivery partners, who sell and service your product. In the case of SAP, that partner activity makes up about 80% of all their annual sales activity.

If you have a product, such as an IT system, which could be sold by a partner, you will want to explore this as a sales channel. Partners, for many vendors, are their secret sauce to success. For example, Hubspot[31], the provider of my company's Sales and Marketing system, sells most of their projects via partners.

They came to this model after trying different approaches to their market. What they eventually concluded was that the deals that were sold and serviced

---

[31] Hubspot, Stock Symbol, HUBS, is a provider of Inbound Marketing and Sales Software.

via partners were far more likely to result in high customer retention than deals where customers bought straight from Hubspot.

What they also discovered was that though their initial product was aimed at, and priced for, extremely small businesses, the real sustainable market was higher up the food chain, that being businesses with at least 3 to 5 million in annual revenue and up. When you dug into their original model, of which we were one of those small businesses, most small businesses simply did not have the internal marketing staff to really learn the Inbound Marketing Methodology. It resulted in very high customer churn.

That's why it's almost always the case in the IT space, especially the SaaS space, that you will find some sort of partner model. It's also why you must diligently think through both your own partnering model and as well, be very selective about which other vendors you partner up with. Both decisions are critical when it comes to knowing and shaping what you sell.

If you really want your partner channel to perform well, then you must thoroughly think about and design the partner compensation model to be attractive. What does that mean in practical terms? It means that both parties must make money on the deal! Every partnering arrangement I've seen that works has meant both sides truly could win.

I have often seen perfectly good pairings go bad because the bigger of the two partners thought they should get a bigger slice of the pie. Many factors, both internal and external, drive this negative behavior pattern. But suffice it to say, you must ensure your partner offer is financially attractive. Or you will find yourself partnerless when you need them. Or worse, you will find your partner is staffing your project with lessor qualified resources and your reputation is getting damaged. Transparency goes a longways here and is one of the hardest aspects of partnering. But it can and must be achieved if you want to make partnering work for your business.

Summary and Lessons Learned

Partnering is one of those tasks that often makes the difference between success and failure. The right partner(s) can help you win in markets otherwise out of reach to you. There are a number of lessons you should take away from our discussion on successful partnering:

- **Partners Open Up Opportunities, When Done Right -** Large IT firms are partner dependent
- **Accountability Is Key for Today's Customers -** Customers want one 'neck' to ring when it comes to partners
- **The Right Partner Opens Closed Doors -** Good partners help you penetrate accounts otherwise closed
- **Partnering Is About Relationship Management -** Managing partnerships can be fraught with friction
- **Mutual Expectation Setting Required -** Signed partnership agreements with detailed performance agreements baked in are a must for successful partnering
- **Keep Track of The Entire Partner Network -** Many partners also will bring in partners to deliver what they do. This is ok, as long as all players are aware of each other and the lines of accountability are maintained

- **Look Under Your Partners Hood -** You must know

your partners true capabilities, not what they wished they did

- **Allocate Time for Partnering -** Large complex projects often require on-the-fly partnering in order to be able to bid. Large organizations have dedicated partner managers. My experience has been that they often don't have the partner I need, so you must be resourceful
- **One Bad Apple Can Spoil The Whole Barrel -** The reputation of your partners is as important as your own firms
- **Make Partnering a Two Way Street -** Good partners will bring you into their deals

CHAPTER FOUR

Dig Deeper

FIND A NEED AND FILL IT

Back in the day, they used to teach salesmanship in high school. Not sure whether they still do, but if they don't, they should. I needed the credits to graduate, so I took the course. It was a decent course if a bit dry. But the key takeaway was "find a need and fill it".

LESSONS FROM A HIGH SCHOOL SALES TEACHER

Build a Better Mouse Trap

That's considered sage advice, if not a bit trite in its simplicity. For some things, there's always an obvious need which anyone can plainly see, i.e., food, shelter, transportation. When it comes to identifying what you will sell or are selling within one of these macro level categories, it can be very difficult to identify what you can sell competitively.

For instance, let's take furniture and in particular, IKEA. In his book, Simplify[32], Richard Koch explains how IKEA came to completely define an entirely new category of furniture, as well as upset an entire business eco-system, namely, furniture. As time went on, the IKEA model reshaped the entire supply chain, which allowed IKEA to provide ever more variety at ever lower prices.

This model has allowed IKEA to crowd out traditional furniture manufacturers. It has also forced competitors to find more efficient ways to manufacture their products. Though there is still a market for hand-crafted high-quality furniture, for the vast majority of the market, IKEA provides 'good enough' furniture for most needs.

IKEA has also been able to vastly expand the available market by selling cheap furniture. Not only is IKEA the supplier of choice to students. It is also routinely the supplier of choice to many other market segments that

---

[32] Rich Koch, Simplify: How the Best Businesses In the World Succeed

would never have considered them in the past. They have been able to provide a winning product to market segments like new offices, empty nesters and even campers.

They have been able to define a completely new market by getting their sales model right. They know what they sell. They must be doing something right, as you probably have something from them in your house or office, even if you don't know it.

How To Find The Need You Can Fill

Though I will jump into the latest fashion du jour, namely Jobs to Be Done or JtBD in a later chapter, I want to cover this subject in a far more practical sense. Namely, find what bothers you[33]. There are many, many businesses out there that exist only because the owner got tired of putting up with a problem and invented a solution.

It's one of the reasons there are so many ways to hold your phone in your car, regardless of the risk this may entail. It's also why your kitchen, if you're aren't careful, can become completely full of gadgets, which probably hardly ever get used.

Here's how I've repeatedly been able to find problems to solve, and reasons to invent a solution. Pain. That's right, suffering both physical and mental pain has often inspired me to consciously look for a solution.

Oh My Aching Thumb

---

[33] Paul Akers, 2 Second Lean - 3rd Edition: How to Grow People and Build a Fun Lean Culture

Here's an example my mother still harangues me about to this day, because she has seen exactly what I invented for sale in the hardware store, but not sold by me. And that is the lowly nail holder. Not just any nail holder, but one I specifically invented for driving tiny little finishing nails.

Why did I invent it? Because we were building yet another family house, and by we, I mean my family. We built everything we lived in and we were nailing old wooden paneling, which also requires the use of dark colored nails. These nails are tiny and are hard to see. I was good at the hammer but had succeeded in mashing by thumb and forefinger into a bloody pulp, on more than one occasion.

To solve this, it was very simple, I took a piece of scrap paneling, drilled a small hole just big enough to snugly hold the nail in place, with an escape grove in it, and voila, instant, useful nail holder and pain avoider. You can now find these, made from plastic, almost everywhere. Unfortunately, I didn't patent it, but somebody else surely made a lot of money from them. Proving once again that just having a good idea isn't enough to successfully bring a product to market.

A More Complex Example

Sometimes, a problem requires a bit more ingenuity, albeit practicality still should rule the day. One such problem I was once faced with, was how to get my aircraft maintenance technicians to stop putting stuff wherever they felt like and instead, put it where it was supposed to go.

Not an uncommon problem, I am sure. However, in this case, the problem was a little bit harder due to the scale of the operation I am talking about and the cost of non-compliance. You see, at one point, I ran the C-130 Hercules Depot Overhaul operation line at the SA-ALC, or San Antonio, Air Logistics Center, Texas.

I had about 350 people directly under me. The larger facility, which also provided depot overhaul to B-52 Stratofortress Bombers and C-5A Galaxy cargo airlifters, had about 2500 people working at the same location. The base, which also overhauled jet engines and performed thousands of other tasks on hundreds of thousands of components, had almost 35,000 workers, and employed an army of contractors in addition to these 35,000 employees.

The problem was and is, people are lazy. They don't mean to be, but physics dictates that we all want to do as little as possible. When it comes to working on airplanes, there's a concept called Foreign Object Damage, or FOD. It is caused by jet engines injecting metal parts that shouldn't be there (and anything else that shouldn't be there, like frozen chickens).

But, as I said, people are lazy. In addition to the issue of jet engines injecting F.O. (Foreign Objects) and incurring FOD, we had one other, huge, on-going, could not be solved, pull your hair out, get yelled out by everybody problem. That was not putting parts you had removed from the airplane in the proper parts storage area, which were basically bins on wheels that sat beside the airplane.

The problem came when we moved the airplanes from one location to another during the maintenance cycle, which, for the B-52, we did an average of 17 times during a nine-month overhaul period, sometimes many more times. Whenever we moved one of these aircraft, someone needed to tow these bins from wherever the aircraft was to wherever you just took it. There were usually between 12 and 17 bins per aircraft. A bin, by the way, was about the same dimensions as a full-size pickup and could, when fully loaded, weigh thousands of pounds.

The problem was the design of the bins. They were just open top boxes, on wheels. As you put parts in them, you were usually just stacking parts on top of parts. Soon, if you were a mechanic, you were forced to continuously remove parts to find the part you needed to complete your task. It was far easier to find a part[34] just like the one you

---

[34] There was a procedure for 'legally' swapping out a part from one aircraft to another (k-balling, canning). When followed, to the letter, eventually, a replacement part would be procured by Supply. Eventually. Between the hassle of this system for swapping parts, and the much easier 'midnight' requisition method used by mechanics, i.e., grab a part that fits, a hole was created. Once created, this hole would travel from one airplane to the next. Sometimes, this hole might stay in existence for years or even decades. Sometimes, the hole might 'jump' to a foreign Air Force that flew the same airplane. A hole was highly resourceful. It would do almost anything to survive. It would hide in Supply. Sometimes it would disappear only to reappear somewhere else.

needed, in somebody else's part bin.

Which they did, with abandon. To the uninitiated, this should be no problem. After all, the parts are the same, they have the same part number. But, au contraire, they are not the same, not the same at all. In fact, the vast majority of the surface parts, i.e., outer skin, are cut-to-fit parts, meaning they are trimmed to fit that particular airplane.

There was one other source of F.O. throughout the facility - flat surfaces. Like dust bunnies in your room during basic training, 'things' would just magically appear on any flat surface that existed, anywhere within the 17 square mile work area that made up this particular depot.

Simple Solutions Are Best

Looking at those bins, they reminded me of a tiny warehouse, in fact, they reminded me of a closet. Just a poorly managed one. If you spend any time in an industrial facility and become intimately familiar with OSHA and its way of thinking, you will know that their basic rule of the road is, if it is possible to design the problem out of existence, then you are obligated to do so. And I did.

I turned those boxes with open tops into closets with wheels. And then I provided heavy duty hangars, i.e., metal hooks, and aircraft ID placards, and made them towable. It became, basically, a box with no walls and no floor, on wheels. With plenty of metal hooks for hanging

---

Sometimes, a hole could be filled by a part from a totally different type of aircraft, if you happened to know where to look and were 'flexible' with your sourcing operations.

parts from. Then I had all the old bins destroyed.

I used what I could from them. But given the cost of a single destroyed jet engine from FOD, it was a good deal. The entire project took about 2 months. There was grumbling about the hassle of using the hooks at first, but we soon eliminated lost parts, which was a source of many of other problems.

Still, this was release 1.0 of my solution, and I still had the flat surface problem, though I had not recognized it as such, yet. I also started noticing that even though my bins were now working much better, and were actually reducing the number of lost parts, people were still able to throw junk on them, even if they had to be creatively lazy to find a flat surface to do so.

Then, one day, while facilitating one of my QCs or quality circles, which was part of our base wide Total Quality Management initiative known by the acronym QP4, I had a brainstorm. I had noticed that in one of many production lines, we used inclined surfaces to allow part transfers from one workstation to another. Seems simple now, but it wasn't then.

As I had many, many sheet metal mechanics, machinist, and other specialist under my command, I put together a flat surface elimination task force. SHET for short.

As my boss, a full bull Colonel had always advised me, it was better to ask for forgiveness than for permission, I began a massive effort to install sheet metal on all flat surfaces throughout the facility. Yes, people thought I was a bit crazy, but they didn't take long to understand what I was doing.

I eliminated every single flat surface that I could find anywhere on that 17 square mile airfield. Those closets without wheels, little pieces of slippery sheet metal did the trick.

Bases of light poles, wrapped them in funnel shaped sheet metal. The walls of the hangar, which was the 2nd largest building in the world, check. Ground Support Equipment, or GSE, check. Everywhere I could find a spot, I put the team to building my little Tee Pees. Soon, the problem was eliminated.

But then, a new problem appeared. Now that there was no good flat surface to put stuff, people would just lay it down. But it turned out to be because we didn't have many garbage containers in the facility. Easy enough to fix, but it turned out to be harder than the rest, because you needed someone to empty them. That was done by contractors, which meant dealing with the contracting office.

Eventually, my simple solutions to a fairly complex human behavior problem paid off and I got the place cleaned up, at least somewhat. That's the lesson of this case study, find a problem, find a solution, try it. Learn from it, solve the next problem. It's how you find a need and solve it.

Summary and Lessons Learned

Finding a need and filling it is very sound advice. The challenge is to find the need. The solutions are usually fairly simple, if somewhat difficult to implement. There are a number of lessons you should take away from our discussion on finding a need and filling it:

- **Find the Problem Like a Detective -** Relentlessly focusing on finding a problem is key to finding a problem worth solving
- **Pay Attention to Your 'Gotchas' -** If it bothers you, it probably bothers everybody else
- **People are Complicated -** Many problems are caused by complex human behavior
- **Know What OSHA Says -** If there is a way to design a solution to a problem to eliminate the possibility of errors, then you should, indeed, you must
- **Cross-Pollination -** The solution to the problem facing you is often a matter of using a solution from some other part of your life or your expertise
- **Keep Drilling Down -** Solving one problem often uncovers the next problem
- **Hard Problems Are Often Valuable -** The next problem is often harder and more valuable to solve
- **Simplicity is Difficult to Achieve -** Complex problems may require complex solutions, but the true value lies in finding simpler ways to solve problems

- **Better Solutions Still Require Marketing to Win -** Though it may be true that if you build a better mousetrap, they will beat a path to your door, the truth is, many better mousetraps have been invented, yet were never properly marketed and failed in the market
- **Use All Your Problem-Solving Tools -** There are many methodologies for uncovering problems. One of the most popular is the 5W or five why's method. I personally like to use Mindmaps. I also recommend the use of many of the quality management tools, such as Fishbone diagrams, SPC tools, Taguichi methods of experimental design and others. Serendipity plays a role as well. The biggest challenge is to simply find the problem

CHAPTER FIVE
Real Insight

JOBS TO BE DONE AS A METAPHOR

Products Get Hired To Do a Job

When it comes to figuring out what you're selling, Clayton Christen, author of numerous books, including "Competing Against Luck, The Story of Innovation and Customer Choice", has done an excellent job of introducing the concept of Jobs to Be Done or JtBD into the lexicon.

JtBD is all about finding out what a customer hires a product to do. There are many examples out there of finding out that why someone buys something is different from why the seller thinks the customer buys.

For instance, in their research, Clayton and his team found that customers were buying milkshakes for breakfast. Didn't really make sense. So, they observed people for a considerable period of time buying milk shakes for breakfast. Then they interviewed them as they left the store where they bought the milkshakes.

Turns out that they were buying the milkshakes to consume on their way the work. They took a while to consume due to their thickness. For many consumers, the amount of time it took to consume the milkshake was about the right amount of time to occupy them during their morning commute. The milkshake was also very convenient, as the straw rarely dripped and thus, did not mess up their clothes. Who would have thought of a milk shake as a breakfast food, which it clearly is not.

COMPLICATED BUT USEFUL APPROACH

A Useful Method - But Expensive

In my experience, this approach works, but is complicated to do and expensive to pull off. You're going to need to observe customers 'in the wild' and then talk to them. Customers are notorious for telling you what they think you want to hear. That means you'll need to observe and interview a statistically valid sample size to draw valid conclusions.

The challenge is identifying what the actual job is that a consumer is trying to get done. Going deeper, you'll need to make assumptions about what that job is. It is not always clear to the person you're talking too what the real job is. That means there's some real artistry in using this approach effectively.

A Real World Example

It is not often that I have been the subject of one of these JtBD studies, but there is one area of my professional life where this actually happens fairly constantly, and that is user research being conducted by either Google or Facebook.

As I currently manage many millions of dollars of Google Pay-Per-Click (PPC) advertising for clients and similar amounts of Facebook advertising and to some extent, Amazon advertising, I am often asked to participate in user research. They often pay me for this, and what's even more interesting to me, is that, at least in the case of Google and Facebook, I have often seen changes made to their system that seemed to address my concerns.

How do these user research interviews go and how do they qualify as JtBD type interviews? In most cases, that's actually what they sort of call them. They will ask me to log into the advertising system (Google Ads[35]) and then ask me to walk them through my workflow, a fancy way of saying, show us how you use our system.

Unless you're an experienced Google Advertiser, you may not appreciate the complexity of this process, nor of using their tool. But, as of the writing of this book, there are at least 31 different types of ads you can create with Google Ads. Within each of these ads, there are many, many options to decide upon.

But knowing how to use their ad tool is only a small part of what you actually have to understand to do this like a professional. First and foremost, you have to know what you sell. If you can't sell it face-to-face, you probably won't have much luck with Google Ads. Then you have to know how you're messaging works, usually on your website, and how it aligns with what people are looking for. You find out this last part using Google's keyword planner.

There's also a huge number of tracking codes to install, conversion actions to set up, other systems to set up and integrate, and then there's the ad creation process. I don't want to make it sound Uber complicated, but the truth is, it is. Google makes a lot of money it shouldn't and wouldn't if everyone was a Google Ads ninja.

---

[35] It used to be called Google Adwords

What Areas Have They Focused On

In my experience, so far, this process usually consists of one hour or so of structured questions. They do not tell you in advance what they are actually focusing on, but instead, usually lead you there by asking questions about something in specific they are interested in at some point during you performing a task, like setting up a particular ad type, or creating a conversion action.

There is almost always a two-man team, one for taking notes and one for asking questions. Sometimes it is only one, and they record it, but the better, more deeper conversations come from the two-man team approach. They've had me walk them through virtually everything I do to set up and manage an account, and as well, how I use their other properties, such as YouTube or the now defunct Google+ social media network.

Often, they will ask for follow-up interviews, where they will dig further down into what I am trying to do. I find it interesting as I used to do similar work, which I will now delve into.

Database Design User Interviews

For a long time, I worked as an Oracle Designer 2000 Master, designing Oracle Databases and custom software. The process we followed was called the Oracle CDM or Custom Development Methodology and the tool we used was called Oracle Designer 2000, CASE[36] Tool.

---

[36] CASE = Computer Aided System Engineering

Basically, you could design a highly functional Oracle Database by drawing process models inside this tool and hitting a button. You still needed to know some PL/SQL to create final versions of the software you were building, but for the most part, it was ready to run, good enough software.

But to get to that point, of being able to design those process models, you had to conduct structured user interviews. In one of my projects, this involved me and my team traveling around to all of the different airbases in Saudi Arabia, where I was working as a contractor. At each base, we would interview everybody in maintenance and supply, from the base commander on down.

These interviews resulted in a series of process models, which were all carefully created from our user interview notes and generated using the CASE tool. This was very, very expensive to do, and to my knowledge, no one else in any Air Force, including the USAF, had ever created a complete set of fully documented, completely integrated set of process models for maintenance and supply using a CASE tool.

From all this activity, we actually did learn exactly what everybody was really doing, versus what the governing regulations[37] said they were supposed to be doing. There was often a huge distance between these two concepts. We also were able to use this information to update those now obviously out-of-date regulations to reflect reality.

---

[37] Governing Regulations: In this case, it was primarily Air Force Manual 66-1 that we were using as source documentation.

The point of this little case study is to point out that investigating what people are actually doing or using a product for is nothing new. It has been going on for a long time and will continue well into the future. The question is, what tools you will use, how much will it cost you to do it, and what useful output can you derive from this analysis. But do it you should.

Summary and Lessons Learned

Understanding what people are actually buying a product or service to do is a key challenge to your success. There are a number of lessons you should take away from our discussion on Jobs to Be Done:

- **Get Firsthand Information -** Observing your customers in the wild will yield better information faster than anything else you might do in your research
- **Ask Why 5 Times -** You must keep asking why to really understand why customers buy a product or service
- **Find and Use Proven Methods and Tools -** This type of research, in one guise or another, has been conducted for a long time
- **Be Creative with Method Selection -** There are a variety of methods to conduct this research
- **Match Research Cost to Expected Value -** Chose your methods carefully, make sure they match the value of the eventual output
- **Beware of Too Much Automation -** Automated tools, like CASE tools, are useless unless handled by trained experts
- **The Truth is Out There -** Keep in mind that most, if not all of your potential customers won't really know the hidden, underlying reason why they buy a product

- **A Good Idea is a Good Idea - Sometimes -** Not all 'demand' can be uncovered this way. Sometimes, you got to take a chance on a product that isn't clearly being asked for by customers[38]
- **Be Persistently Consistent -** It's important to be consistent when conducting user interviews
- **Video or it Didn't Happen -** It's also, if you get permission, very helpful to not only have a good note taker but to film interviews for later analysis.

[38] Henry Ford is thought to have said that if had asked his customers what they wanted, they would have said a faster horse.

CHAPTER SIX

Battle Field

ARE YOU SELLING BUSINESS-TO-BUSINESS

People Buy From People

Selling to a business is both different from and yet the same as selling to a consumer. The more complex and expensive your product or service is, the more complex your sales process is. This complexity is induced from both the seller and the buyer.

On the seller side, the complexity comes from the fact that your product often requires a huge amount of input from the customer before you can actually price it. For example, when it comes to pricing out a complex SAP ERP system, an area where I have extensive hands-on experience, it can be very difficult to figure out what the customer needs.

Part of the reason this is so is because SAP, like many other IT systems, has many, many modules, and solutions. Some modules do what they do in a stand-alone mode, while others work together to support end-to-end business processes. A customer's business processes are almost never known by the same name as the IT system[39], i.e., SAP.

Another complexity comes from the fact that customers often have their 'requirements' nailed down, but want the vendor to suggest alternatives, which intimates a deep understanding of a particular customer's business

---

[39] Within the SAP space, you will often hear terms like P2P or Procure-to-Pay. Though they make sense, unless a client is already on SAP, it is highly unlikely they refer to such a process internally.

processes. In order for a vendor to acquire this deeper knowledge, time must be spent analyzing the customer's operation. In some very rare cases, customers may be willing to pay for this process, while other times, they want it for free.

Dealing With 3rd Party Auditors

Yet another challenge comes from the customer wanting to have independent 3rd party validation of both their business processes and of potential solutions. Though a good idea, in theory, practically speaking, these exercises are typically conducted by very junior people with little to no background in the solution providers solution.

The net effect of this independent 3rd party investigation and validation of requirements and solutions is usually cursory level understanding of what is required and available. If you're a vendor, this presents a huge challenge to you. But there's probably not much you can do to avoid this often conflict-ridden process.

Focus on Value

But there is plenty you can do to make sure you win the deal. It comes down to knowing what you sell and what value you bring to the business. For very complex systems, that means knowing how to prepare a business case, based on ROI or Return on Investment calculations. The more you can do this in an automated fashion, and the more 3rd party validation you can get for your business case, the better.

WHY BUSINESSES BUY

Why Businesses Invest Not Spend

Now that you know a bit about the complexity of selling Business-to-Business or B2B, it's time to dig a little further into the reasons a business buys new products, services or systems. Though a business also has Jobs to Be Done, when you get right down to it, a business spends money to make money.

That really means that, unlike a consumer, who buys something that they generally are going to consume and will have to make more money in order to buy more, a business is spending so it can make a return on investment or ROI. Think about the implication of that.

Though there are literally hundreds of KPIs or Key Performance Indicators a business may focus on, profitability is generally right at the top. Profitability is a lagging indicator[40], meaning you only know what it is after the fact. Cash-to-Cash cycle time is a much more relevant predictor of future performance, and something producers focus on.

What is the Cash-to-Cash cycle time? Before I provide a simplified definition, it helps to agree upon the fundamental purpose of a profit-making business - that is to run a dollar through the system, and when you get that dollar back, have it include some profit. For example, if

---

[40] The exception to this rule is when you prepare your business plan, where, with a system like SAP Profitability and Cost Management, you do, in fact, plan out your target profitability. There's no guarantee you will make it, but at this level of planning, you're generally running a very tight ship and are among an elite few of businesses.

you are making 35% gross profit, when you put a dollar into your system, you expect to see 1.35 cents back at the end of your Cash-to-Cash cycle time.

This calculation is easier for a product maker than a service provider to calculate, because one carries physical inventory, while the other typically does not. A service provider, of which there are a huge number of them, sells man-hours. Every day, they essentially create 8 hours of inventory per worker. At the end of the day, they've either sold those hours or they have not. If they have not, they suffer a 100% loss on those hours. If they have sold them, they have to have sold them at a high enough rate to cover the salary, business overhead and profitability requirements to make their business model makes sense.

For other service providers, such as high-end consultants, which is the space I position myself in, the goal is to avoid per hour charging. Instead, the goal is to sell based on value, while productizing some of the more mechanical parts of the process and finding someone who can do it 'well enough' for less than me, and hand it off.

ARE YOU SELLING BUSINESS-TO-CONSUMER?

Consumers Can Be Picky

Selling to end consumers, also known as B2C selling, is something every consumer experiences as a buyer every day. It is a highly complex market, with a nearly infinite number of products and services available to meet every consumer need. It is also ever more difficult to pull off.

The difficulty in this sector arises from many factors. The first, and perhaps most challenging to understand, is the sheer number of new products being introduced every year. It is estimated that there are between 26,000 and 28,000 new consumer products introduced into the market every year. Fewer than 100 survive and of those, perhaps 1 or 2 ultimately enjoy long term success, where success is defined as consumers wanting to keep buying it.

If you want to see an example that proves my point that many, many items are introduced to the market, yet do not survive, visit a restaurant called Cracker-barrel. Make note of their wall decorations. It is essentially a museum of products from the past. Though it is possible to still buy many of them, what you see is what used to be, not what currently is.

The need that each of the products you can view in that restaurant still exist, yet in all cases, a new product has come along to fulfill the need and pushed the old product aside. I find it interesting that many of the featured 'antique' products are related to farming and the outdoors in general, reflecting the agricultural past of our society.

Now that I've provided you with a handy roadmap

down memory lane, let's switch over to the retail behemoth, Amazon, where I've accumulated 1,000s of hours of experience setting up digital stores across a wide variety of product categories. What do you see here? Everything, as it calls itself the everything store. And you can find a lot in here, though not quite everything you might imagine.

If you're going to have a successful product, you're going to need to master Amazon. But this book is about knowing what you sell, not how to set up and run an Amazon store, which will be covered in another book in this series. What you need to learn from selling on Amazon is that you can find what to sell with Amazon and a whole universe of 3rd party tools available to perform market research.

One of the easiest ways to use Amazon when you're exploring the market is to use the search function. It will tell you a lot simply by typing in the letter A in the search bar and looking at what the smart drop-down list suggest. You should also look at the Amazon 'Best Sellers' list as that's a pretty clear indicator of what is currently in demand.

There are other tools out there that read the Amazon API and give you information about the number of products being sold, one of which I like is AMZScout. The reader should be aware that any information this tool uses is not 'exact' information, but is rather, intelligent guessing. Nevertheless, I've found plenty of good product ideas using this tool.

But retail sales via digital channels such as Amazon aren't limited to Amazon, not even close. There's still an entire universe of physical stores out there, despite the retail apocalypse[41]. There's also a universe of retail service providers, such as accountants, lawyers, doctors, hairdressers, and junk haulers. The list is long of all the places and ways you can make a buck.

In our digital marketing and sales practice, we've helped business owners in just about every one of these categories and many more, improve sales and profits. Much of our success helping such business owners has come down to helping them refine and focus their offer, in short, making sure they know what they are selling and what the benefit is.

For instance, one of our clients was building a sensor that would measure how well you were hitting the ball in hand ball. It was very high tech and we found it very impressive technology wise. However, there was no known customer demand for this product. So, we helped them both improve their product and to 'discover' the customer demand. What they found was that what people actually wanted from the product was the 'competitive rush' from winning. Hard to measure that with a sensor, but you could build an app which measures how much better your swing was. Which is exactly what they did. That product is now available and doing well in the

[41] Retail Apocalypse: The name given to the current era in which thousands of long-established retail stores are being shuttered due to competition from Amazon and other newer channels.

market.

The lesson here is that long before you go investing R&D dollars, spend a lot of time getting to know what your customer really wants. For instance, I grew up helping my dad drill water wells. From one perspective, what we produced was a hole in the ground. If everything went well, there would be water in that hole, and in many cases, that was exactly what we found.

In many other cases, we didn't find water and the customer was disappointed. But the customer really didn't care where his water was coming from, he just wanted water for his house. So, there was an opportunity to sell many of the competing solutions to water wells, for example, cisterns or ponds. These were less desirable solutions, as you either had to buy water to replenish the cisterns, or you had to deal with fairly complex filtration systems to make the pond water potable.

By understanding the overall goal of our customers, we could suggest many solutions, and we often did. There was and is no real way to see under the ground and find water (other than 'witching', which, though entertaining, may not actually work), and the geology of our customer's land was complex and it was mostly down to luck if you found water. If you couldn't find a good source of water, the land wasn't worth much. And city water was not available in most locations and still isn't. So, it was a fairly substantial market opportunity.

Many of our customers were small business owners who desperately needed a source of water for their business to operate. For example, farmers are small business owners, and need water for livestock and crops. Some farmers, for instance, hydroponic lettuce growers, need substantial quantities of very high-quality water in order to grow their crops year-round.

OR BOTH

You Have to Talk To People

Not to state the obvious, but a business, per se, doesn't buy anything. Nor does a robot. People buy everything. That's why, despite the fact that you may have engineered your sales process down to nth degree, the business which needs your product still insist on you talking to someone in their business.

I've worked on projects that dealt with very high order volumes, largely in an automated fashion, yet still, people were making the decisions. The automation that was used there was a Kanban tool, but the 'trust' had to exist between humans to make it all happen.

Trust Comes First

Trust, as it turns out, is the second most valuable asset in business. The first is a buyers (or consumer, depends on what you want to call them), decision to buy something. But the buying decision is always preceded by establishing trust. Trust in the brand, trust in the product, trust in you.

Trust is not easily obtained, yet it is easily lost. Trust is one of the foundational elements necessary for ecommerce. Without it, nobody is going to pony up their credit card and hit that buy button. In B2B sales scenarios, where transaction volume via electronic means is ever rising, there has to be trust not just in you, your product and your brand, but in the entire infrastructure that allows a business to purchase from you.

But when it comes to large, complex sales, I think it is

worth repeating a bit about my background in SAP and especially, in SAP Sales. SAP software is a large, complex beast of a system.

To price it out, as a Senior SAP Industry Principal, I had to use what was called the SAP Pricing Tool, which had over 1,300 items on it which could be considered in a given pricing scenario. There were many, many more solutions available from SAP Partners which I could and did include in proposals when it was required to meet the customers' requirements.

A Complex Sales Process

For most SAP sales, the process goes something like this: an RFP (Request for Proposals, sometimes preceded by an RFI or Request for Interest) is issued to the market, a Discovery Session[42] is conducted, a Pre-Sales Demonstration[43] is provided, a contract proposal is submitted and finally, a deal is signed between SAP and the customer.

That's a highly simplified view of the process. Now I want to expand on each of these steps just a little bit, so you can see why you're actually selling people-to-people at every single stage of the process.

Initial RFP Stage

The truth is, if we were responding to an RFP, we were

---

[42] A Discovery Session is when a Pre-Sales consultants sits with a business user to understand their actual requirements versus what is written in the RFP, which often times is vastly simplified from what is actually needed

[43] A Pre-Sales Demonstration can be conducted either on the system or from recordings made by the Pre-Sales Consultant. It is highly recommended to use recordings. Live demo's go South and there's really no upside to them.

already in a weaker position. An RFP is a complex document, typically consisting of a long list of required features and performance specifications. Many companies do not have an internal capability to create these, and even if they do, for instance, they have a procurement department, it won't have the skills to specify all of the requirements of every department in the company. In fact, not even the IT department will have this capability. To solve this shortcoming, they may hire a 3rd party, such as Accenture, IBM, CapGemini, BearingPoint or any of dozens of others that exist in the market.

These 3rd parties are supposed to bring a measure of objectivity to the process of writing an RFP. Perhaps, in some fairy tale land, they once did. But the truth is, they are limited by what they know about available software, like SAP and by what they, themselves, know about the company they are supposed to create these RFP requirement documents for.

Thus begins the process of requirements definition, and where the first people part takes place. For you see, word gets around, and smart players, aka, SAP, learn to network with these independent 3rd party companies to make sure they are fully aware of the capabilities of SAP.

Other times, (and this is where, in my role as a SAP Industry Principal, I often played a role), the company will ask SAP to do the requirements definition exercise.

We would typically take these roles on with the expectation that the software selection is a done deal, while only the implementation partner remains to be selected. This is sometimes the case when a venture capital[44] firm is buying the firm and mandating the use of SAP and thus, it isn't a competitive situation, but rather, finding those requirements so we could prepare the SAP Software License quote.

This is the ideal situation for a company like SAP to be in - they are on the other side of the table with the prospect working as 'trusted advisors'. It may sound a little incestuous, but in reality, if it is done right, meaning done by people from within SAP with very deep knowledge of SAP, then the result is usually fairly balanced.

Once these requirements are gathered, regardless of who does it or how, the next step is the 'Discovery' session. What's a discovery session? Well, even though the company may have paid someone to develop an RFP, again consisting of perhaps thousands of lines of requirements on a spreadsheet, you still don't have information to do a software demonstration.

In order to do Discovery properly, this is where the next big level of trust building comes into play, which is between the various members of the Pre-Sales Demonstration team, and all the various members of the different departments within the customer organization who can speak on behalf of the customer.

This process can take a while and cost a lot of money to do right. But it is also where the vendor, i.e., SAP, will begin to develop rapport and trust across a wide swath of the organization. This is critical, because although one

---

[44] CEO's Guide to SAP

person will ultimately say yes to the purchase, many people can say no and kill the deal.

ROI Can Be Controversial

In these complex engagements, in addition to doing these Pre-Sales Discovery Sessions, there will also be teams of people working on developing a business case, using commonly accepted factors, such as ROI. Of course, most customers want to push back on all ROI[45] calculations. The higher the projected ROI of the business case, the less negotiating power they will have at contract closure. Sounds bad, but it is my lived experience.

Once the Discovery Session is done, the Pre-Sales demonstration sessions are delivered. These are either live or most likely, pre-recorded walk throughs of the SAP software showing how it performs each of the business scenarios detailed out in the RFP.

There will be an evaluation committee attending these sessions, including the business decision maker from each of the concerned business departments, ideally the same ones that were involved in the Discovery Sessions. The evaluation committee will usually have a copy of the RFP with SAP's answer on them and they are validating our answers.

Aside from demonstrating the software to prove it can

[45] This may sound counter intuitive, since, in many people's experience, they will have been asked to prepare an ROI calculation for any project they may have pitched when they worked internally in a company. But from a negotiation stand-point, customers neither readily share legit information with vendors nor ever readily trust "'Profit Proposal's" made by vendors. However, they are often swayed by these in the background and remain well worth the effort on the part of vendors.

do what we said, we will also be 'adding value' by showing what it can do that isn't on the RFP. What does that mean? And how could we be allowed to color outside the lines like that? Simple, most well written RFPs, meaning not landmines set by the competition, invite bidders to do just that. It takes time and money to write an RFP, and without exception, they are not perfect representations of what is required. But most vendors have a lot of knowledge about how other customers operate.

So, a railroad monopoly in Egypt is more than anxious to hear how the Deutch Bahn (German Railroad) operates. After all, they've been running on SAP for decades, are many times larger than Egypt Rail and most importantly, as members of the Rail User Group, have shared their requirements over the years with SAP and all the other rail users who are members of the user group, and thus, are more than willing to share their 'lessons learned'.

These Pre-Sales demonstrations require a great deal of preparation and rehearsal to do right. Today, there are a number of books on how to demonstrate, the most important of which is Demo2Win[46]. When I started in SAP in 1999, there were none, at least that I could find. The main thing to know is that there are proven techniques for doing this right, and ways to blow it. It is as much about theatrical presentation skills as it is about technical and business acumen.

One Quick War Story for Perspective

---

[46] Robert Riefstahl: Demo 2 Win! The Indispensable Guide for Demonstrating Complex Products

If you're one of my many SAP Partners reading this, you've probably heard me tell this one before. For everyone else, I thought this little vignette might help put this Pre-Sales Demo process in perspective.

One of my prospects, who ultimately became a client, was called Egyptian Rail. Though they had originally issued a decent RFP, which I had answered, it was way too vague to be of much value when it came to preparing our demonstrations. Although initially adamant that they had prepared a 'pristinely perfect' set of requirements and we should just demonstrate to it, after many meetings, much tea, and not a few meals that included us evaluating Belly Dancer candidates for a hotel (don't ask, just part of the process), I had convinced them we needed to do a much more in-depth discovery process.

We proceeded to do that, across several weeks, as well as across Egypt in various locations. Keep in mind, this was a very old Railway system, with people still working train crossing lights in places, while other parts of the system were more modern. After a while, they were pressing us to do the demonstration's. But the truth was, we couldn't get to a final vision of what they needed.

Did I mention I was an SAP Industry Principal in charge of the Railroad Industry in the Middle East? In that role, one of the key tools in my Sales Brief Case[47] was what

---

[47] Sales Brief Case denotes an actual digital 'brief case' which was populated with the documents I theoretically should need to run the sales process from top-to-bottom for any of my industries. I found it somewhat useful, but every document in it required customization every single time and there are no assistants to do this for you. These types of systems often exist in other systems with varying levels of functionality. For example, Hubspot CRM has a

is known as the Industry Solution map. Since SAP takes an Industry Specific Solution approach, they have a map of all the different Rail Industry Business Processes, which also shows how each SAP solution maps to and provides coverage of these various processes.

These Rail Industry Solution Maps are editable, meaning I could rearrange, add to, and delete from them. I could also show where we were going to position a partner solution to fulfill a requirement and as well, where we offered no solution coverage and would need to find a solution.

Still, despite all these tools, all the meetings, all this tea (I love Arabic tea), we could not get to an agreement on what was to be demonstrated. So, I went out on a limb and said I would demonstrate the entire SAP Solution Map for the Rail Industry. All of it, every block on it, top-to-bottom, left-to-right.

You Committed Us To Demo What?

The client was at first shocked, as was my Sales Director, that I would make such an offer. I have to admit, I was a bit nervous making such an offer as well. After all, I had never seen the entire industry solution map demonstrated for any industry, let alone an industry we had not closed a net new deal in for almost 30 years. We already owned the Rail industry and primarily sold extensions.

---

functionality called Sales Playbooks, which provide readily accessible Sales Presentations and other Sales Enablement materials useful for sales.

So, it was game on. Back to Dubai, my then home base, I went. I knew this might cause some push back internally, but surprisingly, after I explained the situation 'up the chain' the entire organization sprang into action. This would be the demo to end all demo's, the assault on Normandy beach of demo's.

We asked for and got about 2 months to prepare this mega demonstration. It would ultimately consist of 32 'blocks[48]' and would take three solid weeks to deliver. That means my team and I would spend, in addition to the 2 months of demo build time, six weeks rehearsing. Rehearsing? Yes, I had a 'golden rule', we rented a hotel conference room, and I had the person who would do the actual demonstration deliver it to me.

This goes far beyond 'sell me that pen'. Each and every word must be scripted, rehearsed, and rehearsed again. We video taped people. I was a total asshole, oops, demanding director. But I knew my audience, and I knew my team could, would and must rise to the occasion to nail this one.

I also knew to expect glitches. After all, this was not my first rodeo. I have delivered, in one capacity or another, almost 200 Pre-Sales Demonstrations over the years. SAP had, after many years, finally developed an approach to these that made sense. I was just following their process.

Finally, it was time for the big event. The normal Middle East protocol would ensue, meaning they would be late, interrupt, change the schedule, all par for the course.

---

[48] A block in this case, is roughly equivalent to a scene in a movie.

You learn to deal with it.

And for three weeks, we delivered gold. When it was done, there was no doubt. There was also no competitor left on the field. We had delivered a demonstration of everything on the SAP Railroad Solution Map. We had recordings of every demonstration.

Now it was time for the final step-get the contract signed! First, I had to nail down the scope of the project, prepare the software license quote, initiate the hardware sizing and procurement, get final agreement on the value case, and most importantly, get the implementation proposal ready from our partner.

At this point, the lead person on the deal was the Account Executive (AE). The AE plays a key role in every deal, being the primary person responsible for ultimately getting signature on the contract. But before we got to contract signature, there was still some selling to do.

During the sales process, which stretched across 18 months, not atypical for large dollar SAP contracts, we were also executing a series of parallel tactics as part of our overall sales strategy. One of those tactics was inviting key Egypt Rail users to the SAP Rail User Group meeting, which, during this time period, was holding its annual get together in Ft. Worth, Texas.

If the Egyptian Rail system could be characterized as needing some upgrades, the U.S. rail system, at least at the HQ of BNSF, where we went for the Rail User Group meeting, could only be characterized as 'over the top' eye watering, corporate showy.

Everything about the place screamed well-funded, well managed, and high tech. ID badges, with digital photos and bar codes, prepared on the spot, check. Well-appointed conference rooms, with wall size screens, check. But, to my client, most strikingly, was the lady who came in prior to starting the meeting and gave a safety briefing. I had forgotten about those. No such thing ever occurs anywhere in the Middle East.

The entire process was, as usual, highly choreographed, with plentiful food and drink, break times that people followed, and an audience that did not interrupt the speaker. All unusual behaviors for my guest to observe. But it wasn't just the event and venue itself that made an impression. It was America's infrastructure, despite all the bad things you hear about it.

The first thing he encountered which seemed to impress him was when he landed, his rental car was ready for him as was mine, and he experienced how well that process works. Many may complain about their experiences in the US, but it is a little smoother than most people experience elsewhere. Even in Europe, you run into glitches. Ever try to find SAP headquarters on a GPS in a rental car in Germany? First, you have to know what state it is in, because there are at least two Waldorfs. And if you look at the SAP Corporate Website, it doesn't reveal the state.

The second was the hotel. In the Middle East, as an expat, I've only ever stayed in five-star hotels. Then there are all the rest. Let's just say, they aren't up to the standard you typically encounter in a normal chain hotel in the states. People notice. We knew they noticed.

Get the Right People in The Room

While getting a couple of the client's key decision makers to the SAP demonstration was important, a second major part of the complex sales process is getting the right people from our side to the table. That means Executive Level presence. The higher the better. This was the second part of our parallel strategy which was to bring in the Managing Director of SAP MENA as well as Board Level members of SAP. That's why they own the corporate jets. So we can put them in front of large, potential Net New License sale clients. And they can speak "C" to "C" or CEO to CEO. It's a question of protocol and honor.

Ready To Close

Finally, with all these elements in place, the AE was ready to present the final proposal. Even here, the deal was not done. Remember, there were many elements to this soon to be enormous project. There would be hardware acquisition, software acquisition, training, change management, implementation, and on-going maintenance. There would also be, unbeknownst to either side of the deal, major infrastructure upgrades required in the building where the hardware would be installed, as well as with all of the networks and PCs and other IT infrastructure. All of this is fairly typical, and usually amounts to about 20% of the cost of the overall project.

But we did run into one interesting 'glitch'. The building where the hardware was going to be placed was old, really old, so old in fact, it was registered as a historical antiquity with the Egyptian Government agency that manages that and the exterior facade could not be modified without approval, which was proving hard to get. This would not have been an issue had we not needed to put the hardware on the second floor. To do that, well, it was going in on the second floor, and you could not just carry it up the stairs. It was going through the hole in the wall we were going to knock in it. That was a problem.

So, a bit more budget had to be found and as most problems go, it eventually got solved.

After all this, the implementation could proceed. Which it did, even during the Arab Spring.

Why Tell You All This

Though you might think all I've just done is explained how you sell SAP, which is true, I've also demonstrated that despite the process taking 18 months, and involving many, many people, what we were selling went far beyond a software solution.

Of course, we did sell software, many millions of dollars' worth of it. We also sold hardware, because the hardware was procured using the SAP Quicksizer tool, which ultimately leads to an order being placed with the co-located hardware vendors in Germany.

We also made sure our partners got plenty of implementation work out of the deal. That means they had revenue coming in to reinvest in their business so they would be there for us on the next deal, which is critical to SAP's success.

We also set in motion a series of monthly and annual support payments, because SAP software comes with an annual maintenance bill. As well, there was some training time in there as well. There were other elements to the sales, such as networking and desktop infrastructure upgrades.

But to really appreciate the full, spectacular impact of what this one sale had and understand why we were willing to invest so much into it, you have to think big. You see, this deal was a deal with a government agency, in this case, the Egyptian National Railroad.

It was our chance to prove to them we were serious, to

meet all their bidder requirements and for many other agencies to hear about us and perhaps take a look. You see, that three week 'dog and pony show' was attended by members of every Egyptian Government agency imaginable.

And like clockwork, the opportunities started flowing in. Suddenly, they invited us to bid on SAP work for all their commercial airports, and there were a lot of them, 27 at the time. Then they invited us to bid on work on all their commercial Sea Ports, and there were a lot of these as well, I believe 32 in all. Then, all of their toll road infrastructure, which I didn't even know they had any of. But they do, and they own an enormous number of real estate plots typically occupied by retail establishments. Finally, we were invited to work with the Egyptian Metro system and public transport system, in general.

But this effort did not go unnoticed in other countries, either. We had always had some role or another on various national committees at different points in the past, with me usually being assigned to represent SAP at them. This had been the case when I first joined SAP in 1999 and the Oman government invited us to be on their national EDI standards committee.

Out of the demonstration, first came an invitation to participate in the Jordanian Transportation Infrastructure Standards Committee. Then an Oman standards committee, and then another to a Saudi standards committee. There are many of these committees, and not just in the Middle East. For example, my boss was a key player in the European Smart Meter standards body.

But on an even higher meta scale, the reason for investing so much money in this one mega deal was the railroad expansion plan in existence for the Middle East and North Africa, which extends from Turkey to Morocco. You see, every country, regardless of political status, is facing an ever-expanding population, all of whom need to get around. And rail will be a big part of that process. As well, there is an ever-increasing need for cargo transportation services, by road, rail, sea, and air.

One of those rail opportunities was raising its hand in the UAE, where a brand-new railway was being proposed. That's right, a greenfield cargo railway was being proposed, which has now been built and is in operation. I was invited to speak to them in their 'start up' temporary office in Abu Dhabi, which I did. Though it took a while, the same basic process took place, and they are now a SAP customer.

And those recorded SAP Railway Demonstrations? I started getting request from other SAP offices for copies from all around the world, even SAP China.

One More Large Sale Example

Most of my experience hasn't always involved leading such large-scale demonstrations. In many cases, I've been part of somebody's else team. The 'war story' I want to tell next is about playing the role of SAP Sales and Marketing Director for an SAP Partner who was participating in one of these mega SAP demo's simply so you have a different point of view of how these sometimes go and what the outcomes can be.

In this case, it was only about a two-week demonstration, but it was a demo that came after nearly two years of a Systems Integrator, otherwise known as an SI, performing requirements analysis. Somehow, after all that time, the SI did not have an RFP, or at least one you would expect. Like all demonstrations, ours was preceded by a Discovery Session, during which we uncovered 'much pain', not uncovered by the SI.

By the way, I say always, but take that with a grain of salt. Originally, the request, delivered almost as a demand or fait accompli, was to 'just demo our solution'. This is where it helped to have worked for what I call the mothership, which meant I knew their sales process, step-by-step. So, I said, as the Sales and Marketing Director, sure, be glad too, when can we do Discovery, because we don't demo 'in the blind'. The SAP Partner was quite shocked when the SAP Account Executive simply said, of course, wouldn't dream of having you do a demo without doing Discovery, nor we will do one. And we all ultimately conducted extensive, probing, Discovery sessions.

Our Discovery session was both a good and bad situation all rolled up into one big fur ball. It was good, because we now knew more about what business requirements we needed to demonstrate to, at least as far as issues. It was bad, because it demonstrated the youthfulness of the SI's team, a not an unusual situation, as they really aren't in the business of putting extremely experienced, industry specialist on a single site for years.

After our demonstration, we had our work cut out for us. To truly demonstrate what the client wanted, without doing the entire project, we had to configure enough, but not too much, of the specialized SAP add-on system we specialized in. That is typically highly paid SAP consulting work, and we were working at risk, meaning SAP had not cut us what is known as an IO or Internal Order, a device they can use to pay for services themselves, but which they try to avoid if they can squeeze the partner, i.e., us.

We neither went first nor last in this demo, but instead about halfway through, not an ideal position from a Sales Strategy situation, but one which I could not change. Luckily, our demo went great, though the post-game analysis revealed many areas for improvement. By the way, if you can, always record your demo's and do a post demonstration analysis. Learn from it, profit from it. Trust me, you'll thank me for telling you this.

What Was the Outcome of This Effort?

As with the Egyptian Railways Dog-n-Pony show, this Pre-Sales Demo also had both direct and indirect outcomes. During the demo, which was conducted online (due to COVID), using a tool called Microsoft Teams, we had both a presentation platform and chat to answer questions.

Those questions are the Gold you get from doing demo's. This particular demo generated many, many questions, none of which had been surfaced during

Discovery nor during the previous two years of work by the SI. Though I could answer most of them myself due to my SAP background, some required further investigation, which meant we would have another shot at answering them, and reengaging with the client.

As before, this demo was attended by high-level representatives from various companies that formed part of this seventeen billion in annual revenues behemoth of a company. And as before, they turned out to have additional projects that they needed help with. In other words, the demo has echo's that reverberate throughout the playing field, no matter where you deliver it, or how you deliver it.

We also got some nice demo recordings to use in our own marketing efforts, which saves us a lot of marketing content development dollars. But probably the biggest side effect was that now, we had an SAP AE who knew us, and knew for her next prospect, she could and would pull us in.

Wait a minute, why would she do that versus calling in people from her own side of the house? This is where it gets complicated but basically, no matter how big SAP is, they never seem to have the resources available to fully support you, the AE or the Industry Principal. Yet they have a Sales Quota they have to make, or they're gone.

Inevitably, they are forced to rely on trusted partner resources to make the sale. Companies like SAP are well aware of this. It turns out, it's ok to rely on partner resources, but somewhat risky. SAP has a Sales Methodology they follow, as does just about every other company. They would like for everybody in an engagement to follow the same methodology, but that simply isn't what happens most of the time.

The Parts of The Whole

I previously laid out the basic flow of an SAP sales process:

- Prospect Issues RFP
- Discovery
- Pre-Sales Demonstration
- Contract Proposal
- Deal Signed

Because I cannot teach you every single minute detail of every single step, yet I need to explain the important parts of each of these steps, I am going to dive a little further into some of the supporting elements of this process. I believe it is ultimately critical to understanding what you're selling, especially when it comes to the complex sale.

Prospect Issues RFP

An RFP, sometimes preceded by an RFI or Request for Interest, has many defined purposes on the buyer side, chief of among them is to generate interest from multiple bidders. Theoretically, you should get the lowest cost this way or the best solution to your problem, but probably not both.

An RFI also has many functions but primarily is used to

see if anyone in the market is interested in proposing a solution. From a vendor standpoint, responding to an RFP is both an opportunity (you're in the game) and potentially a waste of time. Ask most senior SAP guys, or Oracle guys or Microsoft guys about responding to an RFP and they won't have anything positive to say about doing it, in fact, most have been trained to say if you're responding to an RFP, you've already lost the game.

Though possibly true, it's also the case that for many scenarios, an RFP is unavoidable, for example, much government procurement requires an RFP[49] be issued, an answer to be received in a certain, highly prescribed way, and opened publicly, and evaluations be public and documented.

RFPs are also used extensively to weed out the little guy from even bidding. For instance, in most large construction contracts, an industry characterized by an enormous universe of small contractors and a few mega size contractors, RFPs for large dollar contracts have onerous bidder bond requirements, oftentimes requiring the bidder to put up the entire expected value of a multi-million or even multi-billion-dollar contract as a performance bond, which eliminates all but the richest and most financially able bidders from even bidding.

Many RFPs have a price, which must be paid by a prospective bidder, even to get a look at them. This is not a

[49] There, of course, many exceptions to this general rule. In a pinch, the USG has been known to issue no bid contracts to someone who they know can get the job done. The Defense Acquisition Regulations provide a lot of wiggle room.

small barrier to entry. What all this boils down to is that many opportunities are simply not open to small vendors.

For all these reasons and many more, I never agreed that responding to an RFP was a bad thing - in fact - it may be the only way you get a chance to be in the game. If, on the other hand, you can figure out how to sell a product that can be easily consumed directly, thus avoiding an RFP, then you probably should. But just keep in mind, some doors open while others may close.

Discovery

This is perhaps one of the hardest tasks to execute well. It requires you to not only know exactly what you sell, it also requires you to be able to ask questions in a very intelligent, probing and revealing manner. This is never a job for junior members of your team. You will not get good results and the client will know you didn't send your "A" team.

In my experience, the best Discovery sessions result from having structured questionnaires, Senior Consultants doing the interviewing and having the guy the customer can't afford to break free being the subject of the discovery interview sessions.

One thing to keep in mind about doing Discovery is that it is very expensive, for both you and your customer. It takes time, often uncompensated, but yet paid for by somebody. That's why I always recommend you conduct highly structured interviews. Leave the open-ended interviews for another time.

Pre-Sales Demonstrations

When you get to this stage in a sales cycle, you have a lot invested in the prospect. That's why this is where you must take the time to rehearse your demonstrations. Rehearsal needs to include 'hard questions' and hostile and friendly audiences. Yes, this is a major time burner, but trust me on this, when you are selling 7, 8 and 9 figure deals, you will need to make this investment if you hope to win it.

Contract Proposal

The more complex the deal, the more time gets burned here. If you sell large dollar, complex systems, I can't overemphasize enough the need to set up a bid team, if not an organizational bid center. There's nothing more wasteful than seeing an Account Executive writing complex contract documents versus being in front of the customer closing the next deal.

The big 'thing' here is to have developed templates, gotten the legal issues pre-baked into the contract documentation and to make sure the expensive, senior level people are spending their time reviewing the documents for commercial viability (meaning will it win), and not crafting documents.

You should also focus on making your proposal beautiful, and I don't just mean esthetically. I mean it should follow well-trodden layout examples, and be very clear who needs to do what, what it will cost and probably most importantly, make sure nothing is left to doubt about how and when payments will be made. I have had clients refuse to pay because our payment terms did not coincide with their internal terms. Something they neglected to inform their CEO about when he signed our proposal. We got it sorted out but created friction on an otherwise highly successful project.

Deal Signed

It's a big deal when you finally get to signature on a contract, whether large or small. But here's where you have to make sure you have the next steps clearly delineated and ready to execute. Nothing worse than going through the nightmarish sales scenario I've just described, only to have your company's reputation besmirched by stumbling here.

Summary and Lessons Learned

Understanding who you are selling to and what you sell is critical to success. The larger, more complex your product or service, the greater the number of people you will be selling to.

- **People are Key -** People buy everything, whether you know it not. Purchasing departments are abstractions, it's people in them who make the decisions. And they usually are responding to people above them, i.e., CIOs, CEOs, CMOs, CFOs.
- **Large Deals Cost a Lot to Pursue -** Complex sales processes require significant time and investment. There are exceptions to this. For example, people make enormous purchases of Google Ads, and have basically, zero ability to dictate to Google the Terms & Conditions. Unless you're a Google, you will have to navigate through the thickets of the typical complex sales process for high-end products and services
- **The Key Decision -** Though trust is hugely important, the decision to buy something is even more so
- **You Will End Up Answering RFPs -** RFPs are both friend and foe. They aren't going away. But they can be automated
- **Learn to Ask the Right Questions -** Asking customers what their actual business requirements are or conducting discovery, is not to be taken lightly

- **Make Full Use of Everything -** A well delivered demonstration oftentimes leads to other opportunities, so record them
- **Professionalize Your Response Production System -** If you respond to a lot of RFPs, set up a bid center. At minimum, keeps copies of all inbound RFPs and your responses. Build that library
- **Get the Right People Doing the Right Jobs -** Don't force your sales people to spend time preparing proposal responses. On the hand, since they will oftentimes have to present and close, they have to internalize the structure and content of your proposals
- **Learn from Past Efforts.** Use templates to speed up proposal responses and improve win rates

CHAPTER SEVEN

The Big Why(s)

WHY CONSUMERS BUY

The Importance of Knowing Why Your Customers Buy

Knowing what you sell is valuable, but of little value if you don't why your customer buys something. Oftentimes, for smaller, day-to-day purchases, such as when someone buys groceries, it appears that the only reason someone buys is based strictly on price. Though this may appear to be true, one has but to look around at all the different retailers selling what are essentially identical products, but at different price points.

As you move further from purchases at the consumer level back up the production chain, you start to find buyers (your consumers if you're in B2B) who buy for a bit more than price, though price is always a key decision criterion. For instance, a buyer may buy to acquire a new production capability, or simply to replenish a raw material required for production. For commodities[50], such as corn or coal, price is set by 'markets', yet variation is still present in both source of supply and actual quality of supply.

Let's dive into the three macro level reasons that people buy something:

- Need
- Emotional Fulfillment
- Status Achievement

[50] Though the dictionary definition of commodity, "a raw material or primary agricultural product that can be bought and sold, such as copper or coffee" may cover some commodities, the actual meaning of a commodity goes much deeper. A commodity, such as copper or coffee, has known, agreed upon characteristics and when you buy it, you often 'buy against the standard". But there are many other products and services that can fall into the commodity category, while, in the professional services space, many skills are called commoditized, but upon closer examination fail to meet the definition of commodity. If you think a skill is a commodity, ask yourself if there is any risk at all of the outcome being variable. If there is, you're not dealing with a commodity skillset.

NEED

Where Is The Need

I define need as having a clearly defined reason to buy something. It may be to feed yourself, or it may be to move up the value ladder. It may be to get something useful done. If you think about Maslow's hierarchy of needs, there are various types of needs at different levels of the hierarchy. Whether you agree with Maslow's Pyramid or not, I don't think it's hard to imagine that many needs fall into the lower part of the pyramid, those being the Physiological (food, water, warmth, rest) and the next one up the pyramid being Safety (Safety and Security).

The remaining part of the pyramid, the next three levels, Belonging and Love needs, Esteem Needs, and Self-Actualization, all have different needs associated with them, with regards to products and services someone might need.

When it comes to businesses, it is a little harder to neatly package their 'needs' into such a hierarchy, though you can benefit from trying, when you are defining what you sell.

When you get right down to it, the major difference between how an individual expresses a need and a business expresses a need, it is that a business usually is fulfilling a need in hopes of making more money from their investment, while an individual is fulfilling a need and usually is not expecting make more money from it[51], at least not directly.

Within these two broad categories, business vs consumer needs and the observation that each consumes for different reasons, there is quite a bit of grey area or counterfactuals. For instance, school in all its flavors.

When Demand Exceeds Supply

In this area, i.e., schools, of which I have experience both setting one up and as well, helping clients boost sales of an existing school's courses and planned ones, there is a clear expectation by a consumer to get a financial return, just not directly from the dollars invested. I mention schools specifically because they represent a major exception to the rule that consumers are spending money to fulfill immediate needs.

Schools (including any kind of training) are unique. You attend a school in hopes of being able to earn more in the future, but there are no guarantees. Yet most Universities have more applicants than spots available. They therefore have to have a way to sort out 'applicants'; some would say supplicants.

It isn't just higher education that is able to generate more demand than supply and thus ever higher prices. In places, such as New York City, the pressure to get into the right school starts early, way earlier, in pre-school, often with parents starting the application process before the child is even born.

There is no known immediate financial payoff for

---

[51] Of course, the other exception are things like investments and property.

attending a high priced, highly selective pre-school, except for one; it is the only route into the next level of school, private elementary and high schools, and eventually, elite selective universities, such as Harvard or Princeton.

Is what is being taught in these schools of a higher quality than other institutions? Possibly. But experience says that the network is far more valuable. Networking is how these institutions add potential future value to their graduates' lives.

Leverage Network Effects When You Can

There's a lesson in this for anyone hoping to leverage network effects[52] for his product or service. For example, switching back to the physical product world, let's talk about athletic shoes again. Within that world, where we have considerable experience, there are competitors at every price point and in every niche. Yet some shoes sell for $20 dollars while others sell for $800. That's a result of many factors, which are discussed in other parts of this book. What's more interesting is that many such shoes are far more valuable on the secondary, collectors' market. In fact, these types of collector edition shoes have spawned an entire sub-culture of shoe collectors and even an online marketplace.

The shoe itself is used to generate bragging rights among the cognoscenti. But these bragging rights are only

[52] Network Effects: The idea that the more people use something, the more valuable it is. For example, a phone is useless if only one exist. If 2 exist, it is more useful, but barely. But if everybody on the planet has one, i.e., mobile phones, then network effects kick in and the device is far more valuable.

valuable if there is a network of other collectors, to whom outsiders can only stare and shake their heads in disbelief at the prices some of these shoes are now garnering.

In the case of one of our customers in this space, whose shoes had been worn by celebrities in Music Videos, Movies, and TV Shows, there were collectors who had every single model ever produced and had standing orders for any new models, even if not in his size. The collector, of course, was only too happy to post unboxing videos on social media, and to this day, keeps buying and telling everybody who will listen about his collection.

This type of product aficionado exists across a huge variety of product categories. There are people, primarily men, who have every type of woodworking tool imaginable. But within that product category, there are high-end 'professional grade' tools, and then everyday tools. One gets used, the other gets collected. Yes, those high-end tools are generally very high-quality tools, but the price premium, often several hundred percent, isn't justified by just having a sharper blade which last longer. It's a result of network effects from the collectors, the same as the shoe collectors.

There are too many examples to list them all in this book, nor would that be valuable, but I will mention just one more, so that you have a flavor of what's possible and where product possibilities exist. That is in the area of heavy equipment, specifically (only because I grew up working on one) Bucyrus Erie heavy equipment. It has its own Facebook Collectors group[53].

I specifically grew up working for my dad, a water well driller, and we owned and still own a Bucyrus Erie 20W Cable Tool Rig used to drill wells. It is very old technology; this particular one dating from the 1930s, as far as I know. But it works, just slowly, when compared to new, rotary well drills, first invented in the early 1950s. It turns out, like almost all other pieces of equipment you might want to explore, there are collectors out there who spend their time and money restoring and showing off their Bucyrus Erie equipment, and not just well drills. If you check that group, you will find people who find and restore all manner of Bucyrus Erie equipment, and as before, have joined a network of fellow collectors to display their works.

Now, this type of equipment won't exactly fit on your bookshelf, and frankly, won't fit on or in most properties. It requires massive space, which has value all its own. It also requires people with disposable income to actually restore this often difficult to work with equipment.

It is also a clear example of a product fulfilling one of the higher-level needs on Maslow's hierarchy of needs. That's why it's critical to really get to know your customer when you are designing your product or service, it's the only way to really know what you sell.

---

[53] Bucyrus Erie, https://www.facebook.com/groups/1642565949317656

Summary and Lessons Learned

Knowing what need your product or service fulfills is critical to success. You just have to have thought completely through what you sell. There are a number of lessons you should take away from the 'need' opportunities discussed here:

- **Understand Why Money Is Spent** - Businesses invest, consumers buy
- **Understand the Cash Cycle of a Business** - Businesses invest in anticipation of getting their investment back with profit tacked on
- **Consumers Buy for a Different Reason** - Consumers spend to fulfill a need, but it doesn't often have an expected profit return
- **Exception to a Rule** - Consumers do invest with an expectation of a return when it comes to education and training and investments
- **People Are Buying Ever More Training** - The market for online training[54] has absolutely exploded and is growing year over year at a furious pace
- **Grow Your Web to Juice Usefulness and Profitability** - Products that can benefit from network effects have the upper hand in almost every product category
- **Collectors Are Influencers** - Many products have

[54] Examples: Udemy, NYC Data Science Academy, LinkedIN Training, OpenSAP, MooCs, MasterClass, to name a few well known examples.

collectors that will spend big bucks on their collections

- **Figure Out How to Care For Collectors -** There are innumerable opportunities to provide add-on services to these collectors
- **Dig Deep into The Need -** Some products fulfill a need that a consumer never knew they had until they see the product
- **Consider Niching Down -** Not all needs can be met but if you can find an unmet one, design a solution for it, and get in front of the right person, you can make hay

EMOTIONAL FULFILLMENT

Emotions Drive Sales

While many day-to-day purchases, think ice cream, may be perceived as strictly 'emotional fulfillment' type purchases, they often, also fall into the need category. That said, let's explore some typical examples of things people buy or consume to fulfill some emotional need.

During my time in Dubai, that mega-center of commercialism, there was a clear indicator of an emotional buy - the supercar. I have to admit, even I bought my own little toy, a Mercedes Benz SLK 350, which wasn't very practical, but was fun to drive and own. Though I was quite proud to own my Benz, which I bought in cash, I was put to shame by the Bugatti Veyron[55] that parked right beside me in my garage at The Address (that's the actual name of the place), which mostly collected dust.

Sometimes - Paying More is the Goal

Interestingly, during my search for my car in Dubai, which, as usual for me, took a while, I got to know almost every dealer in the area. What I learned about their customers was an eye-opener. You see, the buyer of the Bugatti Veyron, Lamborghini, Porsche, Mercedes-Benz, BMW, Audi or any number of other high-end cars, at least in that market, weren't buying on price at all.

They typically bought in cash if they were locals. The exception being the cowboys[56] who were there to make a

---

[55] Bugatti Veyron, https://www.bugatti.com/models/veyron-models/

[56] Cowboys (and Cowgirls) in this case, does not refer to cattle wranglers. It was mostly

fast fortune, who often failed, and left these cars at the airport, to be picked up and ultimately recycled. No, the buyers of these cars, were interested in, above all, in having something unique, a model available only to the Middle East, and oftentimes, completely customized by them.

What makes a supercar hyper expensive? It isn't because the performance is 10 times better than its lessor cousins. After all, a Tesla will smoke them at the track every day of the week, without any customizations. No, they were buying to 'see and be seen'.

Seen by whom? Other supercar owners and women if they were men or men if they were women, or both. How do you know this was true, how could you find this out? Because you can find them for sale every day of the week with virtually no miles on them. They aren't very comfortable after all, they are like a woman who wears a too tight dress - looks good, but not very comfortable.

That's why when it comes to knowing what you sell, especially in the high-end luxury market, knowing the motivation of your buyer and aligning that with your emotional messaging is critical. It's also why you absolutely must know what you sell.

Story Telling For Emotional Impact

People are hardwired to tell and listen to stories. We've been, as a species, doing it for tens of thousands of years. The

---

expatriate Real Estate agents, either men from the UK or exceptionally beautiful women from Eastern Europe, normally, highly educated, and anxious to find their fortune.

gifted storyteller has a huge leg up in business and in life. That's why so many of us attend movies, read books, and will spend significant amounts of time listening to other's stories, of woe and triumph, love and loss, struggle and achievement.

One such CEO I worked for was a well-known Latin TV figure. He was in the Health and Fitness space. Most importantly, he had a backstory that he told, over and over again, about being a fat boy who got thin, and how it affected his life. He always told it in Spanish, as his audience was Spanish speaking women in the United States. And they were 99% women, with perhaps six men out of 100,000 being his customer base.

I must admit, even I would get a bit teary listening to him, even after I heard him tell it for the 20th time. It had very little variation in it from one telling to the next, but it did get refined over time. I know. We measured certain aspects of the audience's reaction and refined it and tweaked it to hit them where it counted, in their hearts.

Story Telling Takes Practice

I do not consider or rather, did not consider myself, a storyteller. But now, I recognize that, indeed, I have the gift of gab, as I have been told over the years, perhaps by people who didn't quite want to listen any longer. I did not consider it a skill at all long ago, let alone one you could improve with practice.

For instance, when I first joined the USAF, I was sent on an expenses[57] paid trip back to my home in Indiana as a recruiter's assistant. The goal of my trip was quite simple, discuss my experiences within the USAF with my circle of friends. To do that, of course, I had to tell stories. I have never been shy and was glad to invite my friends to canoe trips, pizza and movies, and anything else I could dream up that we liked to do and which the USAF would pay for on my expense report.

I found myself being the storyteller, while most everybody else was more than willing to listen to me. It felt kind of strange, but I guess that's why the recruiter wanted me on this little adventure - tell the story, sell the service. Perhaps a few signed up because of this, but I could never prove it, nor was I asked to try.

An Officer is Always Selling

Later on, in my USAF career, after I had gotten my degree and my commission as an officer, my story telling skills would be put the test on a regular basis, only with much more purpose than before. Unlike the image most people seem to have of the military of a place where an order is given and an order carried out, it really takes a lot more than that to make things happen.

Though I could probably fill a book with 'war stories', or so my daughter would claim, there was one event that I think is worth mentioning, because it was one where I had to tell a story that was designed to invoke a sense of urgency and pride, one of those emotions that must be managed carefully when you're selling your vision.

---

[57] Paid by my employer, the USAF, i.e., American taxpayer.

In this case, the story was simple. We were facing an existential threat to our base and most importantly, to our aircraft. The threat came in the form a major hurricane, in an area where we hardly ever experienced major hurricanes, San Antonio, Texas. At the time, I was the Deputy Commander for Maintenance of the C-130 section at the San Antonio Air Logistics Center, or SA/ALC, Kelly AFB, Texas, located on the South Side of San Antonio.

To put the scene of my big speech, aka, story, in perspective, you should know that our flight line covered a 17 square mile area, consisted of one of the largest buildings in the world, and numerous other buildings. That was just the depot maintenance area for the aircraft we worked on.

The larger base had hundreds of buildings and employed about 35,000 people on any given day. It was also one of the largest military supply depots in the entire defense department.

We performed depot maintenance on C-130 Hercules tactical air transportation aircraft, B-52 Stratofortress Bombers and C-5A Galaxy cargo transports and occasionally, OV-10 Broncos. At any given time, we would have about 17 B-52s in the center, 30 C-130s and 5 C-5As. Most would be in some state of disassembly; of most relevance to this story, many did not have their landing gear installed.

The day of this story, I had gathered my people together, and laid it out to them - hell was coming our way. We needed to get every single aircraft into one of the hangars. We could not fly any of them out as we would normally do and as I had done on other occasions at other bases getting hit by a hurricane. We needed to get them secured. And we needed to do it within the next 48 hours. There could be no failures. Our aircraft, aside from being amazing pieces of equipment, were of strategic national importance. The loss of any single one would be a severe national security incident, greatly endangering national security.

From the end of that brief speech, which lasted no more than 15 minutes, because every second counted, my people, all twentyfive hundred of them, burst into action. We jacked up gigantic C-5As, installed temporary landing gear and rolled them into the hangar[58] and tied them down.

We had dozens of C-130s without wings or landing gear, sitting on demurrage[59], all over the place, due to the wing replacement program they were undergoing. We installed wheels on the demurrage stands, we installed skates when we could and we used cranes to move the rest, all into the same gigantic building.

Then we had the B-52s. These eight-engine beast were a lot trickier to move, especially as most were structurally unable to be moved due to a modification we were doing to them to carry ALCM[60]s. We spent a few minutes with

---

[58] Our hangar was specially modified to accommodate the C-5A's extremely tall tail and horizontal stabilizer.

[59] Demurrage is a term you frequently hear around shipyards, where ships have to pay fees if they are there too long. Why our engineers called our stands this was never made clear. But they did.

[60] ALCM: Air Launched Cruise Missiles. In this case, we were installing rotary launchers which required structural modifications.

my engineering team, came up with a way to cross-brace them, and added more wheels, brought in more skates, and more specialized equipment.

Hand of God Damage

It was controlled chaos. But we got them locked down and under cover. Then, all hell hit. Three huge tornados, spawned by the hurricane, tore across the base, and cut huge swaths of destruction through base supply. By sheer luck, our airplanes escaped damage. From the air, it looked like a giant 'hand of god' had taken three fingers and ripped three channels of absolute destruction across the base.

Not only had the tornadoes destroyed a lot of base supply's physical infrastructure, the vacuum of the tornado had sucked parts off their shelf throughout the complex of buildings, which were so large, they had railroad tracks that ran up and down between them. This would normally have been of little consequence, you just put them back where they belong.

Unfortunately, for a huge number of items, no one knew what they were, nor where they belonged. You see, many of them were parts for aircraft and equipment that were long ago removed from the active inventory, but which allied nations still operated. Part of our support agreement with these allied nations included keeping parts, manufacturing capabilities and trained people to help them to continue to operate these pieces of ancient equipment.

Normally, when Base Supply would run across something in inventory (which happened all the time) that they didn't know or recognize, they would contact us, the maintenance people, to come take a look and see if we could identify it. Not a big deal, a task for which we were normally staffed and equipped to handle. Not this time.

This time, instead of looking at a single item, we were looking at acres of items, intermixed, some damaged, some not. And we were under pressure to get our own operation back in motion.

In short order, inflatable warehouses, supplied by an Air Force Red Horse squadron, sprung up to put stuff in all up and down the supply line. My people, who were also dealing with the destruction of their own homes in many cases, swung into action, and around the clock emergency response recovery operations ramped up.

This was all before the commencement of the first Gulf War. Which is a whole other dramatic story, perhaps best told at a later time. The entire point of this story is that it is, at least in my opinion, an emotional event, one which I have told more than a few times, when I needed to rally the troops, be they civilian or military, to let them know, you can do great things. If you sell, you may find a few of these types of stories handy to keep in your repertoire.

What Was I Selling Here

In the scenario above, I would have to say that what I was selling was a vision of what must be. I identified the enemy. I was ensuring that everybody was onboard with the mission. People want and need to belong to a group, to something bigger than themselves.

Of course, when everything was done and back to normal, a key activity was passing out recognition. The military is typically very good at this, perhaps better than anybody else. But though I was in the military, and an officer, almost all of those 2,500 people I mentioned, and indeed, almost all of those 35,000 people who manned the base, where not in the military. They were federal civilian employees, and unionized. Many were temporary contractors.

Unlike military members, there were very few ribbons or medals to be passed out. But there were plenty of 'Certificates of Appreciation', Public Recognition Events with trophy's, free meals, and even cash rewards (though tiny sums) which I could and did pass out.

I can guarantee you that those written certificates of appreciation are still in existence and guarded closely by their recipients or their families. Many will still be around a hundred years from now.

Summary and Lessons Learned

Knowing which emotional lever to press is a key skill. Used properly, under the right circumstances, you can sell your vision to even the most jaded audience. When it comes to emotional fulfillment:

- **Know Your Audience -** There's really no magic formula here, but if you spend time getting to know your audience, you will eventually come to 'know' them.
- **Stories Build Trust -** If you tell stories with meaning, with relevance to the situation at hand, you'll develop deeper, more meaningful connections to your audience.
- **Simple Stories Get Retold -** If you tell stories often enough, you will eventually hear your own story told back to you. It has happened to me, all over the world.
- **Great Stories Get Written Down and Recorded -** When your audience ask you if they can record the story, as they often do with me, don't be offended. They are sharing it and playing it back among themselves. If you can get a copy of that recording, get it.
- **The Best Stories Elicit Questions -** When your audience ask questions, to go further into the message you're trying to convey, you're doing it right. When you tell a story and you hear crickets[61],

you bombed.

- **With Great Story Telling Abilities Comes Great Responsibility -** When people are listening to your story, be responsible with your story telling. There's a world of difference between manipulation and persuasion.
- **Learn the Story Arc -** Hollywood tells a story with a beginning, a middle and an end. They know what they're doing, and you know when they go off script and don't follow the template.
- **Use the Hero's Journey -** Most great stories have a Hero's Journey, when you use a story to sell, make your customer the hero and let them see themselves in that role.
- **Place Your Product in the Story -** This is one of the hardest skills to master. Don't do it on the fly. Think about it in advance.
- **Use Your Story Against Your Competition** - With Caution. A good story that places you in a positive light while hammering your competition[62], can be done, but go down this path at your own risk.

---

[61] Story telling also has a huge cultural component to it. Foreign audiences may respond very differently than your own culture.

[62] In the case of the African Airline I mention elsewhere, I told a story I could back up, as I was actually a trained, certified and experienced Oracle Designer 2000 Master and had worked on Oracle systems for years. I knew, at a profound level, how difficult it would be to implement their system, versus our structured approach.

STATUS ACHIEVEMENT

Perception is Reality

There are so many products and services on the market, it would be impossible to list them all. However, if you want to seriously get focused on what you sell, then you need to understand what sort of status people achieve or want to be perceived as having achieved, when they buy your product.

Visible Signs of Success

As they say, if you have the cash, you must flash. That doesn't mean you will see people walking around with bricks of cash[63], usually. But for many, there are clear markers of success that they want to display to the world, sometimes deliberately and sometimes only obliquely.

Much of this signaling depends on the income level of your consumer. For instance, if you divide people up into poor, middle class and rich, while ignoring all the minute variations that exist within those broad, general income categories, you find distinct markers of status.

The first among them are kids. It used to be, perhaps 150 years ago in the West, and more recently in poorer countries, that large families were required to work the fields. As wealth increased and education levels increased, birth rates fell, until they reached the current level, which is far below what is called replacement rate, or about 2.1 births per woman, on average.

---

[63] Except in the Middle East, where you actually see this all the time.

Especially in the West, and now most everywhere, the birth rate has declined to well below that level. An interesting phenomenon can now be observed among the wealthy, they've suddenly started having many more kids, while worrying about the lack of births among the middle and poorer classes.

That's because the rich have come to see kids, lots of them, as a sort of status symbol. This is true even when the wife is highly educated, has a high paying job and doesn't need to work. So, if you sell baby carriages, they better be expensive, something to talk about, something that helps maintain the aura of status and achievement.

A second kid related status symbol is attendance at ever higher priced private schools, starting when the kid is still a baby. Many private pre-schools charge more per year than many state universities charge per year. There isn't much difference in the 'Cost to Serve' between a regular everyday daycare and a high priced exclusive private version of the same thing. This is where you have to know your customer, know your offering and segment appropriately.

Finally, there's bragging rights when it comes to kids. How many people are quick to tell those whom they meet what their kids do for a living? For instance, both of this author's kids have done quite well for themselves, one being a 767 Airline Captain and the other being an SAP Consultant, both making a good living in the mid six figure range.

There are other groups of people out there who are

quick to tell you they have doctors, lawyers, engineers, and architects for children, as a sort of badge of honor. If you sell educational services, you should learn to exploit that characteristic among the parents, as they typically are paying the bills on their education and training.

There are other kinds of status achievement that are far less visible to most, yet absolutely critical to the person or business who has achieved the status. Those fall into 2 broad categories, brand power and pricing power. They are closely related in that the first facilitates the second.

Brand Power

Brand power is well known to the general public. It takes the form of visible products people consume and is the result of often years of marketing efforts. For stance, Nike shoes are a powerful brand, with shoes that often cost hundreds or even thousands of dollars. By cleverly using celebrity endorsers, they built a brand that most people just assume is worth the price, because, well, they see the brand every day and they see others paying the price.

That near constant brand presence leads to pricing power. You won't typically see the latest Nike shoe on sale for 90% off. Besides, the person who wears them actually wants to brag to their friends about how much they paid for the shoes.

But there are other, less publicly visible brands out there, but which, nevertheless, benefit tremendously from having a strong brand presence. Let's take one I've introduced to you before, SAP. It's a strong brand, but with plenty of detractors, chief among them competitors setting

FUD[64] traps.

Why do I say SAP has a strong brand? Primarily because of all the CEO's who I know who, though they ask me what is SAP, nevertheless, know that much of their operation both runs on SAP and runs largely without them having to worry about it running.

I've literally been with CEOs of companies that run on SAP who said they wouldn't be the CEO of a company that didn't run on SAP. Sounds crazy, I know, especially since there are many capable competitors out there. Those competitors also have CEOs who will tell anyone who will listen about those products as well.

What the CEOs are really bragging about is the fact that they have working business processes. They know they can get a clear-eyed view of their finances, at a moment's notice. For many, many companies, this is simply not the case. They are run on spreadsheets.

For a truly strong brand, you need to have a product that people are willing to spend far above the product or service's intrinsic value. Want a prime example? The Rolex. It's a watch, of which there are many on the market. Most do a good job of keeping time. In fact, a Timex does a good a job, for about 50 bucks.

But Rolex isn't selling a watch. Not for $80,000 anyway, the price of the one I've worn. They're selling membership in an exclusive, global club of Rolex owners. It signals

---

[64] FUD, Fear, Uncertainty and Doubt

something to others who wear one, sometimes good, sometimes not, but always very visible.

Finally, I want to mention Lexus, the car. Lexus, like the luxury brand of many major car manufacturers, is a branding exercise. But it turns out, it's also a unique car within the Toyota family. It's not just a luxury car, it is considered the most reliable car in the world[65], or at least it was when I bought my LS 460 El Presidente.

I do have to admit, I am a slow, careful shopper, oftentimes taking years to research a major purchase. So, your stuff better be good, good enough to impress someone like me, of which there are plenty. How would I classify myself as a consumer?

Somewhat conservative, given my background, no doubt. After all, I already told you I grew up without running water until I was about 12 or 13 years old. This, even though my dad and I were water well drillers, whose very business was dedicated to supplying water to people. As it happens, there was simply no water to be found on our land, so we hauled it in. Every. Single. Day.

We weren't poor nor were we rich, we were instead, lower middle class. But I was entrepreneurial because there wasn't much money spread around by my parents. I always worked; I always had some sort of business I was running. That translates into an extreme sense of independence and ability to make a go of it, anywhere, at any time.[66]

---

[65] As reported by consumer reports and various car quality rating services.

But I was mechanically adept, having learned a lot from my dad about how to fix virtually anything. But when I joined the Air Force, I became a highly trained aircraft mechanic. Then I became a C-130 Flight Engineer and eventually, after I got my degree, I became a maintenance officer, with a deep expertise in Statistical Process Control (SPC) and even deeper experience in aircraft maintenance, especially at the depot level.

All of that background means 1. I know how to fix things and 2. I really don't want to spend my hard-earned money to fix things if I can find things that are higher quality and thus, require less maintenance. In short, as a consumer, I am picky. If you're selling to me, especially if it is for anything but the most basic day-to-day purchases, and even then, I will have investigated it at some point, your product or service better be the best in the market.

That's pretty much how everybody behaves from where I am from. But it is not how everybody behaves from everywhere. If it was, you wouldn't have people making payments on shoes, as one of my clients, a shoe designer, had.

Which brings me to my final point about status achievement, which is finance. For many people, they may not have the cash to flash, but they could have the status product, if you could provide them with payment options.

And unless you've been buying stuff with beads, you'll

---

[66] I believe it is why I was able to start multiple businesses in Europe, and have worked as a consultant in 38 countries on various projects.

know that there is a tremendous amount of 'power' branding in the finance part of status achievement. For instance, many people have special classes of unlimited credit cards, think American Express black, or whatever their offering is today. For many people who do not get such cards, seeing someone use one of these is cards is meant to invoke a certain sense of envy, while for the carrier of the card, it is meant to convey a certain sense of status while also ensuring they get a slightly easier way in life.

Of course, that's at the high end of finance. At the lower end, there are any number of offers out there, like payday loan lenders, who are there to help those with lessor means buy what they want, even if they have more limited wants, at a price. Sometimes a very steep price indeed.

Show Don't Tell

If supercars are the ultimate male (and sometimes female) visible status symbol, in many parts of the world, jewelry and baubles are the status symbol du jour, if not the emergency store of value for the opposite sex, in those same parts of the world. While in many places, crime rates are too high for women to openly wear expensive jewelry, in other places, especially in the Middle East and South East Asia, gold is often worn in ostentatious displays of wealth. It's just another way to show you have the cash, but in a different form.

The point of knowing this is for you to examine how your product can become an indicator of status achievement. This goes far beyond differentiating your product. It can extend to almost any kind of product or service you can imagine. For example, in Spain, where I currently live, there's a chain of department stores that people shop in because they can then say they shop in that chain of department stores - even when the product is more expensive compared to an identical product in one of the competing retailers.

Summary and Lessons Learned

Positioned as a display of status, many products and services can command prices that bear no relation to their intrinsic value. When it comes to status achievement:

- **Segmented Properly, Your Product Can Command High Prices -** Positioning is a key consideration when it comes to status displays
- **Segment Customers For Success -** It is possible to build customer segments of one. It is harder to build products for a customer segment of one.
- **You Want People to Perceive High Status -** This is a tricky proposition to pull off, but well worth the effort for the right product
- **What is Not Seen, Counts -** What a product does isn't nearly as important as what your customers think it does
- **It Must Do What It Is Supposed to Do -** Even though what your customers perceive a product to do may not be what you designed it to, it doesn't mean you don't have to provide a product that actually does what it is designed to do
- **Businesses Seek High Status Achievement Visibility -** There's a reason why businesses want to make those business magazine list. It brings higher valuations, and ultimately, makes senior management wealthier and possibly, shareholders
- **Status and Emotional Appeal Are Powerful**

Elements of Success - It may not be obvious, but the achievement of status is also an emotional event. Which emotions your client is feeling is something you should take care to model your product around

- **Many Emotions Surface with Status Achievement -** Consumers often feel many emotions when it comes to high status products. Some good, some negative. Each type must be addressed in your marketing and communication
- **Consumers Consult Multiple Information Sources -** It's no secret that almost everybody is researching your product and service before you ever hear from them. Make sure you know what your reputation is 'out in the wild'
- **Competitors Will Also Look At What Your Consumers Are Looking At -** It's a given they will also be trying to cast a shadow on your reputation. Be aggressive about cleaning it up

CHAPTER EIGHT

How Much?

PRICING MODELS

Pricing Models

Pricing your product or service is one of the if not the most critical decisions you will make when it comes to knowing what you sell. The price someone is willing to pay you is dependent upon many things, many of which we've already mentioned, such as status achievement, need, emotional fulfillment, and many others.

There are many approaches to pricing, but I want to concentrate on just a couple, value-based pricing and cost-plus pricing, both of which are very common in the market, but one of which is much more difficult to do than the other, that being value-based pricing. Both of these approaches are usable at all price points and for the most part, most kinds of products and services.

That's a very bold statement, I know, but bear with me, as I try to peel this onion for you. Let's take value pricing, which, to be honest, is both easier to do and more applicable, the higher up the value chain you go. Let's take my favorite subject, software, only this time, instead of using SAP as my guinea pig, let's use i2 Technologies, a supply chain management software company I once worked for.

Of all the companies I've either worked directly for or have supervised (the later includes the likes of Accenture, IBM, KPMG, EY, Oliver Wyman, SAP and Capgemini) i2 Technologies had by far the most advanced, most developed and most importantly, most executable approach to value-based pricing.

What did they have that I have not seen anywhere else or at least at the time, was not yet widely available? They had a publicly facing offer to provide proof of the value their customers achieved by using their product. This 'proof' was provided by a 3rd party audit firm. Their claim to fame was that at the time, in 2001, they were willing to state their customers had saved $75,000,000,000 in supply chain cost from using their software.

But that was only one, admittedly critical element of their value-based pricing approach. The other part was that they had a suite of tools and people available to help build the value case for their deals. The tools consisted of a comprehensive set of KPIs (Key Performance Indicators) that they had arranged in a hierarchy which showed how each drove the other. For every KPI, they had mapped how their software affected the KPI.

The people part of this included a small army of MBA types, myself included, who had been extensively trained on how to use the tool, and how to present the results. This was a major investment on their part, and that training has paid off in my life ever since.

Now, I have previously told you that most clients want to do anything they can to denigrate or lesson the value or ROI of your business case. Again, as a reminder, they want to do this because the stronger your business case is, the less negotiating power they have to drive down your price.

The i2 Technologies counter tactic was awesomely

effective, if exceedingly simple to implement. It was to agree with the customer. But with a twist, and you should do this as well. I will explain this approach by way of an actual customer case I drove home.

We had a chain grocery store prospect, with about 320 stores spread across the north of Spain, where I was based at the time. They were interested in a number of solutions, and we put together our business case, which indicated that we could save them about $100,000,000 in inventory cost annually. They would have none of that.

You see, the hidden message behind such a business case was that their current systems and processes were inefficient, to the tune of $100,000,000, in waste every year, just in this one aspect of their operation. So, they pushed back and beat us up for our assumptions, and when all was said and done, we agreed that our solution would only save them around $24,000,000 in the first year of operations, for an investment of about $5,000,000. They never pushed back on our price.

After the contract was signed and the initial implementation was complete, like clockwork and just as originally projected, the inventory begun to come down, and soon, they acknowledged that we had been right and indeed, not only had they saved $100,000,000 in inventory cost, but they had also actually saved quite a bit more. So much excess inventory had been eliminated from their system that 20% of their warehouse space was now sitting empty.

We were so good at this approach to value based

selling, that even though we faced off against SAP in every deal, we never lost to them. Keep in mind, they had hired me from SAP, so I had the upper hand when it came to understanding their Sales Strategy, which was also based on value based selling, but was, at the time, largely fluff[67].

Often times, SAP would decline to even show up to do their demonstrations once they found out i2 Technologies was their primary competitor. Someday, I will share with you how this evolved into a highly targeted effort by SAP to eliminate i2 Technologies.

This approach to selling based on value is powerful. But it sometimes isn't powerful enough to win the deal on its own. Sometimes, you have to combine value-based selling with risk management. That's when you need a team that knows your product, your sales methodology and has the 'C' suite presence to make it happen. Now I want to give you one more 'war story' about how I led one such project and what I learned.

The scenario was we had been invited to participate in the Airbus A380 program, which was in the initial design stages. They had asked us to first demonstrate our Supply Chain Collaboration software suite. We had done all the normal due diligence[68], qualifying the client, the need, and the timeline, and the authority, and made the business case.

---

[67] At the time, 1999-2003, SAP had not initiated what it now calls Value Engineering. Today, they have a highly refined approach, if often poorly utilized, to business case development capability

[68] This is known as uncovering BANT in some circles.

That only got us to an invite to prove it. This was because what was being asked had never been done before, not with our software, nor with anybody's software, at anytime, anywhere in the world. Nothing like a challenge.

So, my company asked me to assess the project's probabilities of success both from a functional and financial perspective. I did and told them it could be done and was worth doing. Great they said, you run it. We will run it at risk. Meaning i2 Technologies would fund the implementation up front with the explicit agreement that upon successful go live, Airbus would sign the contract, which would ultimately grow to about $25,000,000 in value.

This is not all that unusual or was not at that time. You may have heard of this called a POC or proof of concept, or even conference room pilot or CRP. But the scale of this was far bigger on a spend basis. We were assigned an empty building on the edge of the Blagnac airport, located in Toulouse, France where I began to assemble my team. A team that would ultimately grow to about 35 i2 Technologies SCC consultants and almost 600 Airbus personnel spread across multiple sites.

What made this project unique, at least initially, was that it was about Supply Chain Collaboration or SCC. Airbus had indicated they had about 850 suppliers in our initial data gathering exercise. An SCC project involves connecting these suppliers to the Airbus production systems. Unfortunately, what we found was that about 135,000 suppliers were in the system. Some of this was bad data, while most of it was simply the client not actually knowing how to identify all their suppliers, even having SAP in place[69].

Let's assess where we are at in this little misadventure. We are doing a major SCC implementation with one of the few major global aviation players. We are working at risk. We have found 130 times more suppliers in their database than initially estimated. Time to make it harder, don't you think?

Two weeks into the project, I received a PPT or Powerpoint requesting a CRM or Customer Relationship Management system proposal. It appeared to come from the very top and would have been commercially suicidal to take a pass. We said, sure, why not.

Will You Fall On Your Spear

For the next six months, each Friday, at about 13:00 hours, I was tasked with briefing the CEO and founder of i2 Technologies on this project. And each Friday, he would ask the same question - are we going to make it, and do I recommend we continue. No pressure.

What you have to know about me, that as a highly experienced project manager, is that I depend heavily on my Project Management software. I am a master at it[70], I trust it, and I do not trust anything or anyone else when it comes to managing my projects. My plan, which was by

---

[69] In reality, as they were a company formed from many past mergers, they had many SAP systems.

[70] Others might disagree; of course, however, I have been using it since before it was actually called MS Project.

now, very, very detailed, indicated a day and hour when we would go live.

As the anointed day approached, the tension continually increased. As you might imagine, no one liked the fact that the 'chain of command' was largely being ignored in that Friday meeting. There was little I could do about that except to assuage everyone up and down the Chain of Command with information, which consisted primarily of updates to the project plan, embedded in a PPT.

No Joy In This Victory

On the day the project plan indicated we would go live, we did, down to the minute. I would like to say there was dancing in the streets. There was not. This had been a hellish project. Sales had, in usual fashion, over promised, radically. Heroic efforts had been made on the part of the rocket scientists[71] who built the software to fix the issues.

But commercially, we had met our obligations, defended our pricing and they signed on the line that is dotted[72]. This effort would ultimately lead to many other sales at this client and within the wider European aviation community.

Now, you may not have the resources of a multi-billion dollar software company to undertake such a project at risk, nor even be clear what the value is of your product. But the calculation for determining ROI is available to all,

---

[71] Two of the team members, were, in fact, rocket scientist.
[72] Glengarry Glen Ross. https://youtu.be/Q4PE2hSqVnk

and you need to figure out how your product or service benefits your customer if you hope to sell based on value. If you don't, they will figure out how to get you to a 'how low will you go' scenario in a features and functions battle, and procurement will own you.

Cost Plus Pricing

This approach to pricing is very common and makes intuitive sense to most yet is riddled with problematic assumptions. The very first of which is that you know your cost structure. Here's a secret, unless you have taken specific, repeated action to determine your cost, you don't know it.

Even very large companies, like SAP, have an entire department to determine costs. These departments, referred to as controlling, are key to determining your costs. The problem is, everything they do is based on assumptions that you might or might not agree with, but which are baked into the cost structure.

To position ourselves properly in the exploration of Cost Plus Pricing, I will first have to introduce what may be a new term for you, the idea of fully loaded cost or FLC. If you're working in a company like SAP, for many roles, but not all, you will need to know your FLC rate. Without diving too far down in the weeds on this subject, just know that it is what it cost to put a dollar in your pocket.

There's lots of way to figure this out, but in SAP, you ask controlling, what's my FLC rate, and they give it to you. Let's say your FLC rate is $100 per hour, or $800 a day.

Example FLC Table for a Professional Services Firm (Including Charge-Out Rate)

Annual Salary	$80,000	$120,000	$200,000
FLC	$71.44	$107.15	$178.57
Charge-Out Rate	$100	$150	$250

Breaking Down the Table

At first glance, this rate, is what SAP must sell you for per hour to cover your cost. But that isn't quite the whole story. You see, SAP has to cover overheads, i.e., your boss and his boss, and make their profit, say about 35%. So, let's say that all comes out to be they need to sell you at $150 an hour. That's still not quite the whole story though, when it comes to figuring out what they must sell you for. You see, you also take vacation, attend training and otherwise, spend time that doesn't generate revenue.

The time you have left over after figuring in these factors, is the time you have available to generate revenue. That left over time is commonly called your utilization rate. It will be somewhere around 66% if everyone is honest.

There are a few aspects to this cost and revenue break-down you need to be aware of. First off, your FLC rate depends on not just how much they pay you, but on whatever other costs they decide to load on your position. A portion of your boss' time will be loaded on your position. But so will his manager, and perhaps a portion of many more managers all the way up the chain.

But somebody has to pay for Marketing, Sales and Administration. So, your position will be loaded with a portion of their cost as well. In fact, every cost that can't be covered by selling the software, will have to be covered by your position.

Knowing your FLC cost is the first step in determining what you can sell an hour for, the next step is to add in your profit. Overheads are already baked into FLC in this model. But if you sell to the government, the government may want details of your overheads, so you must be prepared to disclose them. And as one might guess, the government never agrees with either your assumptions about what is overhead nor how much you're charging for overheads.

Next you must add in your profit margin. I am always very transparent with my profit margins, as I have found my best clients not only understand that I have to make a profit, but that I have to make more profit doing what I am doing than I could do elsewhere. The smart ones also know that you 'must' make a profit to stay in business and to be able to provide them on-going, top notch support.

That's why you often see 'Rate Cards' that have Senior Level people at the $450 an hour rate on them. Every hour they cannot bill is ultimately going to be covered by an hour of somebody that is billable. But if they can be billed, they will be.

Now that we have the fundamentals of cost-plus pricing

down, at least for a man-hour, let's explore some of the challenges with this approach. The first is, we have not mentioned the competition. You see, there's almost always someone out there willing to do it for cheaper. You can argue and many do, that those someones aren't the same as me. But your customer doesn't see it that way. If you're selling a man hour that is specialized, say in SAP Material Management, from their perspective, lacking any other data points, they believe their best strategy is to buy the cheapest resource available, as long as the capability is the same.

Another challenge is that the customer has very few tools to determine this, other than perhaps the Brand Power of an SAP certification[73] or having an expert interview the person. An expensive proposition and as it turns out, of little actual value in determining the resources' ability. So, price ends up being the differentiating factor.

Within many fields, actually with all but a few rare exceptions, if you're a buyer, there is intense competition between resources for your business. This is not so complicated when you're trying to get something relatively simple done, say, replace a broken window. But as the size and complexity grows of projects, be they IT or Construction or any other type of large-scale project, then it gets exceedingly difficult to make a choice.

---

[73] SAP Certification and the value it brings is a controversial subject. I personally believe a good consultant should have his certification. I do not see much value in recertification. However, over my SAP career, I have personally taken and passed several extremely difficult, challenging SAP certifications. Contrary to what some say, you can't easily pass them.

That's why you, as a vendor who knows what he sells, better know what he is worth and what value the customer gets from your product or service. That's just table stakes. You also need to be able to differentiate your offering, whether through better quality, price or service if you hope to beat the competition. It's also why knocking out an incumbent is exceedingly difficult yet done all the time.

For instance, I've worked as the Project Director, on behalf of customers, who had entire floors of their building occupied by four or five of the major consultancies - at the same time, meaning they all could and did see and talk to each other, every day. About once a year, this client 'culls the dogs' as they used to tell me, meaning regardless of outcomes, they ejected one of those major consultancies, and replaced them with a completely new one.

That may sound harsh, but these were retailers, and retailers operate like that; as near as I can tell, everywhere. If you're going to play in the retailer space, at least on the systems side, you better have something they can't live without, or you're going to be forced to compete with the lowest cost provider anywhere in the world.

What can't they live without? Something that helps them make more money or cuts expenses, preferably both at the same time. It's not an industry for the faint hearted. But if you do have something they can't live without, they incongruously pay top dollar.

There's one other entity that is more than happy for you to use cost plus pricing, the US government. In fact, many of their contracts require total cost and pricing transparency and only allow a certain percentage of profit. They're great if you can afford to have the bureaucracy to deal with them, but if not, my advice is stay far, far away from them.

Perhaps the greatest problem with cost-plus pricing is the fact that you're probably leaving money on the table. If you're not proving your value, you have little to no pricing power. It's just a question of how low will you go.

Other Common Pricing Strategies

Since we've covered two of the common pricing strategies, value based and cost plus, which I find to be the most common within the industries I deal with, I think you should also know a bit about the other four common pricing models:

- Premium
- Penetration
- Skimming
- Economy

We've already briefly touched on the premium pricing modelwhich is the most common model you see in high status products and services. The other models are also worth considering and each may come into play at different points during your offering's lifecycle.

Penetration Pricing

This one is often used when a new entrant to a market shows up. For example, mobile phones are often priced extremely cheap in new, poorer markets, while mobile phones remain expensive in established markets, such as the USA and Europe. Once the market has been penetrated, and consumer demand has been established, prices are slowly raised until competitors show up.

Skimming Pricing Approach

The get them while their hot approach. High prices are often charged for new products, then lowered as competitors arrive on the scene with lower priced alternatives. The idea with skimming is to charge high enough prices long enough to cover your development and launch cost.

Economy Pricing Approach

This is the no-frills pricing approach. Think store brands, deep discount stores, and other low margin businesses where marketing and sales expenses are minimal. Can work great if you have the volume. I have seen it used in the detergent market where factories in Jordan produced unbranded detergent, identical to branded detergent. Located geographically close to target markets, factories providing products in these segments were operated at near 100% utilization to maximize utilization and capital returns, with little to no sales and marketing expenses.

Their secret to success was to sell only in off-brand stores, where the shoppers had little ability to buy upscale brands. The other aspect of this pricing model is customized package sizes, usually tailored either to be much larger, such as you might find in a Big Box Retailer or much smaller, even down to single use sizes, such as you might find in India for some shampoos.

Summary and Lessons Learned

Getting your pricing right is strategically important to your success. There are a wide variety of approaches to pricing and lessons learned you should keep in mind:

- **Pricing Varies -** I've laid out some of the most common pricing strategies, what you should know is that your pricing strategy can and should vary over time
- **Eyeball Your Competitors -** Unless your offering is completely unique to the market, you should find out as much as you can about your competitors pricing strategy.
- **Your Competitors Will Eyeball Your Prices -** Assume that your pricing is known, even if your prospect signed an NDA in blood.
- **Avoid Pricing Man-hours -** Within the IT space, most contracts are priced either by the hour, on a Time & Materials basis, or by fixed cost. That completely negates pricing by the value you bring. Avoid this approach if possible
- **If You Must Price by The Hour, Know Your Numbers -** Your pricing must cover both overhead and profits. Don't be afraid to share your numbers with your customers. You would be surprised at how transparency can strengthen your pricing power.
- **Fixed Price Must Include Management Reserve on Projects -** You should know and keep in mind that

when a contract is 'fixed price', the U.S. government, which originally defined the concept of fixed price, mandates a management reserve, usually around 20%, be included in the fixed price

- **Experiment With Different Pricing Models -** It is smart to try different pricing models in different geographic markets and customer segments.
- **Know Your Break-Even Point -** This is one of the most common business terms you will hear, but it is difficult to actually compute, and is directly affected by your pricing strategy and decisions.
- **Know Your Contribution Margin -** Like Break-Even, knowing your contribution margin allows you to play with your pricing and fly closer to the sun[74].
- **Understand FLC -** When it comes to pricing out man-hours, knowing your Fully Loaded Cost rate is critical to not underpricing yourself.

---

[74] In Greek mythology, Icarus flew too close the sun and the wax melted from his wings and he fell to earth. In this context, flying closer to the sun refers to being able to charge a lower price and still earn a profit. This then, allows you to be competitive.

CHAPTER NINE

Types of Sales

ONE TIME SALE

For many businesses, you will only get a one-time customer out of any deal. There's nothing wrong with this, after all, it's a 'yes', meaning you got them to say yes to spending at least a dollar with you, which is usually the first step along the path to spending many more.

The challenge is knowing whether what you sell is only ever going to be a one-time sale, or whether there are opportunities down the line to sell more. Usually, I find that customers will dangle the promise of additional sales opportunities in front of a vendor in order to use that promise to negotiate a better deal for this one-time sale.

This is why it is absolutely imperative to know what a customer is worth to you. Sometimes, there's only going to be a single sale between a seller and a buyer. For instance, people who were forced to sell their land to the US government when they bought them out to establish the Brown County State Park, located in Southern Indiana, only had one sale to make and one product to sell.

Most of them were glad to sell what was perceived, at the time, to be hard scrabble farmland, of little value. They were lucky to get a few bucks an acre for it. Today, that same land, were it for sale, would easily fetch $6000 an acre and up. In short, the sellers didn't know what it would be worth in the future, but there were hints all around them that it was worth more, much more.

There are many types of 'one-time' sale items out there,

some obvious, some less so. Day-to-day, people are constantly buying groceries and other daily consumables. They are largely creatures of habits. Meaning if you are trying to introduce a new consumer item into the market, you are up against odds that are strongly stacked against you. That's why most new product introductions fail.

Other Models

There are other models you run across. For example, let's take the example where you need to have some bull dozing work done on a piece of land. Once that work is done, unless the dozer operator has figured out something to 'add-on' to the dozer service, it's one and done.

In general, when it comes to selling something that is a one-time sale, the best advice is charge as much as you can, at least as much as the market will bear, because you're not going to get a second shot.

On the other hand, I've worked with many businesses where we developed creative ways to find something to sell and change that one-time sale into a recurring sale, even if the sale happens many years apart.

One of the more creative ways I've seen someone else do it is converting a one-time datawarehouse implementation into a "one-time" sale plus a monthly service of data validation - to make sure the vendor's datawarehouse was actually reporting accurate information. It's a fairly low dollar effort, with a lot of possibilities for automation, but yet always requiring an interaction between humans (there's that all sales are between humans I told you about) and thus an opportunity to uncover additional opportunities.

I've also seen clear examples, in my experience as a SAP Consultant, of leaving additional sales opportunities on the table. Sometimes, this is because the budget wasn't there in the first place to qualify the opportunity for additional sales. Most of the time, though, it was because the vendor had not done a good enough job of identifying the pain, agitating the pain, and offering the solution, otherwise known as PAS within copywriting circles.

Let's discuss a specific, complex example from a real SAP project I led a few years back. In this case, my team and I had been contracted to deliver an interactive executive dashboard, using a now deprecated technology called xCelsius. We had deep expertise with this, if not with estimating how long the project would take.

In the process of building the dashboard, which involved extracting performance data from across the SAP landscape, we kept encountering indications that the client had problems with product forecasting, and as this was a retailer, forecasting and avoiding stock outages was a major business imperative.

Digging deeper into this problem, we found that the core of the issue was the MRP Strategy being used by the ERP system. There are a number of different MRP Strategies available within the system. The system logs indicated that these MRP Strategy settings had not been changed in ten years. We were able to recognize this problem because I had a material management[75] background and this falls within that domain, partially.

However, the original implementation partner should have set up an on-going service task to periodically check and adjust this setting. By failing to do so, that partner left years of revenue on the table, and no doubt cost the client millions of dollars in lost sales. It was also, from our perspective, negligence to not have periodically checked these settings, both on the part of the client and implementation partner.

---

[75] I am an SAP Certified SAP MM or Material Management consultant. MRP strategies fall within my domain expertise.

Summary and Lessons Learned

There's nothing wrong with a one-time sale. Just make sure you deliver what was promised. This sales model has been around a long time and will continue well into the future. There are many lessons learned from a one-time sale model:

- **Every Sale Is Important -** Treat a one-time sale with as much care and importance as any other type of sale
- **Always Look Beyond the First Sale -** Be careful what you treat as a one-time sale. There are often subsequent opportunities to sell the thing at higher prices
- **Why Yes IS a Big Deal -** You get to yes with a one-time sale. But that is no mean feat. It is turning that one-time sale into a long term, repeat sale you need to strive for
- **What the Market Will Bear -** Pricing is a tricky proposition in a one-time sale scenario. But generally speaking, charge as much as the market will bear and still allow you to win is the best advice
- **Get Creative -** There are oftentimes unexplored opportunities to convert one-time sales into recurring opportunities. You just have to be willing to get creative
- **Budget Gets Found -** Never assume that because there's no budget, there won't be later. The larger the enterprise, the more flexibility they have to find the

budget

- **Business Cases Help Win Deals -** A well-developed business case can help close the current deal and lay the groundwork for many subsequent deals
- **Find the Opportunity For Improvement -** Some call this "find the pain". Call it what you want, but if you connect your solution to the opportunity, it will help your client make a decision that favors your solution
- **Leverage What You Know About Probable Shortcuts -** In most IT projects, and many other types of projects, well known trade-offs will have been made. This is almost always a path that means the customer is operating in a sub-optimal manner. Therein lies your opportunity to re-enter an account
- **Sometimes, One-and-Done Is Ok -** Though you may sincerely believe and have a solution that a client could benefit from, it is ok to just sell them what they want and be done with it. But follow-up, done properly, may yield positive results down the road.

REPEAT

As opposed to a 'one-time' or a 'Subscription' based model, a repeat model falls somewhere in between these two. How would I describe a 'repeat' sale? There are many common examples. However, I think it is useful to differentiate between a repeat customer who buys different products from the vendor versus a customer who repeatedly buys the same product.

In the first instance, a common example is someone who buys many houses using the same Real Estate agent. This type of transaction is repeat in the sense that the buyer is buying a house every once in a while; in the US, that is typically every five to seven years. A real estate agent who does a good job with a new buyer, if they manage the relationship correctly, can count on repeat sales opportunities down the road, possibly for a lifetime. The product is different every time, i.e. houses, but the customer uses the same agent, and thus repeats.

In the second instance, the customer buys the same product over time. You may recognize this as common consumer goods, such as shaving cream, shampoo, milk and other staples of daily life. It can also be expanded to encompass more complex products that are not quite identical but represent variations of the same product. Automobiles fall into this category. A Chevy man may buy Chevy's his whole life, graduating from econobox models to ultimate luxury models over their lifetime.

That's why smart sellers differentiate their products, so they have an offer for each market segment. It's also why

'Brand Power' is so powerful. Consumers are not bombarded with messaging for their entire lives for no reason. They are being marketed too, in hopes of currying favor when the moment of purchase happens.

As you progress up the value ladder, you find repeat customers are especially valuable. Within the B2B space, where product variability is a given, the relationship between seller and buyer becomes paramount to getting repeat business.

For instance, within the SAP space, those relationships are important not just for any particular sale between SAP and a customer. Over time, as SAP has grown in both scope of their offering and in the number of installed base customers, those relationships have moved from one company to the next.

This is the hidden power of the relationship to ensure repeat customers keep happening. It's also a tremendous barrier to entry to competitors. Someone who made their career making the decision to install SAP, isn't likely to take a chance on a competitor in his next company. It happens, but it is rare.

Know Your Customer's Expected Outcomes

From the standpoint of knowing what you sell, this means you not only must know the output of the system, in this case, SAP, but as well, knowing many of the non-monetary aspects of your product and service. In this case, it's our old friend, trust, which is the currency of those relationships that greases the skids for SAP from one client to the next, even when the SAP product is technically inferior.

Of course, with today's technology, like LinkedIn and CRM, it's a lot easier to keep track of those relationships. That why I practice ABC - Always Be Connecting. There's power in the network, especially your personal network. The bigger it is, the more it is likely to display network effects.

What does that mean? It is something akin to the telephone. If there was only one in the world, there wouldn't be much value in the phone. If there were two phones, connected to each other, it would be a little more useful. Now that there are billions of phones, all connected, then the network is very powerful. There's a math formula behind computing this strength, but you already know the truth of this statement. So, grow your network, now and forever.

Summary and Lessons Learned

A repeat sale represents a much more profitable sale. There are many variations of repeat sales and lessons learned:

- **Relationships Rule -** People who have had a positive experience with you are more likely to buy from you again and again
- **Relationships Move Around -** Relationships between people move around from one employer to the next. It pays to maintain those relationships
- **Barrier to Entry -** A strong relationship, wherein a client has repeatedly bought from you and had a positive experience, represents an almost insurmountable barrier to entry for competitors
- **Value Ascension Ladders[76] Unlock Sales -** If you know what you sell, and design add-ons and additional related offerings, you can walk a client up your value ladder
- **Leverage Network Effects -** If you can design your product so that the more people use it, the more valuable it is, you can lock in customers for a lifetime
- **Piggyback Off Existing Networks -** You probably can't invent another mobile phone network. But you can develop a product that takes advantage of it. For instance, how many businesses have been made just

---

[76] Value Ascension Ladder was a term popularized by a company called Clickfunnels. www.clickfunnels.com

from selling iPhone covers

- **10 Times Cheaper Than Net New[77] Sales -** It isn't just a little cheaper to sell to an existing customer, my own experience shows that it is approximately 10 times more expensive to sell to a brand-new customer than to an existing customer
- **Plan Repeat Sales With Your Customer -** For very complex offerings, i.e., SAP, if you're doing it right, you can work with your customer to plan out sales[78] well into the future
- **Collaborate on Value Delivery Roadmaps -** Don't just plan out what you're going to sell to a customer. Instead, plan out how much value, in terms of ROI, you're going to deliver, year after year
- **Be Easier to Do Business With -** No matter what you sell, make it easier to do business with you than your competitor[79]. The larger, more complex your offering is, the more difficult you have probably made it to do business with yourself. Reengineer your complete sales process to overcome this

---

[77] Net New refers to selling to a completely new customer

[78] A tool they use that you should also have a version of is the CVA or Collaborative Value Assessment. It is a roadmap that lays out what additional SAP solutions they should make use of and when. It is closely coupled with a business case.

[79] It is often very frustrating for a customer to get an offer from a vendor. This may be unavoidable, but usually could be made a lot easier if time was invested in truly knowing what you sell.

SUBSCRIPTION

The subscription economy[80] has been around forever, in one form or another. What is a subscription? An example you may be familiar with is the newspaper. You had a subscription to it, and someone delivered it to your house every day.

There are many other examples, for example, your electricity, telephone, water, sewage, internet and even your annual tax bill. Those are the common examples most people are familiar with from their daily life. However, with the advent of the internet and the mobile phone, there has been an explosion in 'subscriptions' in the market.

One of the most famous is the 'Dollar Shave Club[81]', which was ultimately acquired by a bigger fish. It completely disrupted the razor and blade market. It also sent a clear signal to everyone that if you used just a little bit of imagination, you could turn almost any product into a subscription model.

With ecommerce platforms like Shopify or Amazon, setting up a subscription or recurring sale business model, is now technically simple. The challenge is to figure out what to sell on subscription and as well, how to manage the inventory management requirements required to execute a subscription model. This last part of the puzzle is where many have run aground.

---

[80] https://www.amazon.com/Automatic-Customer-Creating-Subscription-Business/dp/159184746X/ref=sr_1_13?dchild=1&keywords=the+subscription+economy&qid=1614262390&sr=8-13

[81] https://www.dollarshaveclub.com/

One such company I worked with specialized in designing high end weightlifter shoes. We had helped the company set up and optimize their ecommerce operations and had steadily grown sales month after month. And month after month, we observed that sales were suffering from a lack of inventory in the right size and style as demanded by the market.

To get a handle on the size issue, and as the owner of what many consider big feet myself, i.e., size 14, we did the obvious, we put up a size survey on the website and asked people what size shoe they wore. This was the only place where we could get this information, as all other sources seemed to rely on guesses and past demand (which isn't the same as knowing what size shoes people actually wear).

Our survey revealed that the sizes were distributed in two nicely distributed bell curves, with women's sizes being centered at the lower end and men's sizes being centered toward the higher end or larger sizes. It also revealed there was demand for larger sizes which we hardly ever stocked.

Our store analytics system revealed what styles were in demand. With these two data points, we were ready to launch our subscription service. However, we had one final hurdle to pass, which, ultimately, we could not overcome.

That was our supply chain.

In this case, as our orders grew in size and frequency,

we began to suffer delivery delays and quality issues. In short, the same problems every company has faced in the past when their supply chain stretches all the way to China.

Using Reorder Point Planning (ROP) and other Industrial Engineering tools, we had determined that our total replenishment lead time was about 8 weeks. And given our monthly demand, we also knew that we needed to reorder every week. Of course, this also meant we had an increase in the amount of cash tied up.

On the upside, we were basically selling out of every model and size. But this ultimately meant we were generating demand for stock we did not have and could not replenish in time to capture this fleeting demand. Thus, we had been leading up to a 'subscription' model, which would provide steady state demand signals to our manufacturing facilities.

There were two problems that we ran into, and which you must keep in mind when you're contemplating moving to a subscription model:

- Our 'sales hook' was exclusivity, meaning our styles changed frequently; oftentimes, we did not produce a run of more than 150 pairs of any one style.
- Subscriptions typically mean people get to choose and pick what they keep and what they send back, which leads to higher returns, a major ecommerce issue.

This is where you need much better data than is

typically afforded by a basic ecommerce store. You need what amounts to an ERP. To get one, you will need to stitch together various applications. You'll need it all to be integrated with your suppliers, which, as it turns out, oftentimes, have no such systems with which to integrate.

Due to all these issues, the subscription model proved impossible to make work. But in many other cases, we've seen it work like magic. One of those instances was with a weight loss company. We were lucky in that they already had a working sales model when they reached out to me, but, like most calls, this one was one of the burning oil platform situations.

My initial assessment revealed that sales had declined precipitously in the previous four months, and were in fact, trending toward zero. However, they had a working sales funnel, and most importantly, a subscription model that made up about one-fourth of their existing sales.

They also had new leads coming in at a rate of about one a minute, which is 1440 a day, and on some days, this number would go to 27,000 leads per day, when we ran TV ads. The first problem I uncovered was that their lead generation system, in this case, Hubspot, had been broken. The previous agency had been full of coders, and coders gotta code. They were not strategic thinkers.

After identifying the list of all the issues, not just with their Hubspot system, but with their Salesforce Call Center, their financial integration with Quickbooks and most importantly, their subscription management software, called Zuora, I came up with a prioritized 'fix it' plan.

Me and my team, and yes, this one required a team, as well as the client's company, quickly started to see a turn around. As this initial list of issues began to get resolved, we were then able to start 'juicing' the marketing with ad spend and most importantly, leveraging Amazon. Though they had a presence on Amazon, sales there had been mostly a rounding error.

On my recommendation, we initiated what Amazon calls Fulfillment by Amazon or FBA. Our shopping cart conversion rate on the ecommerce side was already vastly improved due to our fixes, hitting almost 11%, which is well above what you typically see.

But FBA had a conversion rate well above that, almost 60% on some days. There were days where we were selling 10,000 units of just a single item, whereas in the past, we didn't sell 100 units of all unique SKUs (Stock Keeping Units) combined during the entire month on that channel.

You should have at least a basic understanding of how FBA works to really appreciate the unique power of this channel. FBA basically boils down to you putting your inventory in Amazon warehouse locations around the country. During the process of setting this up and as well, during replenishment, Amazon algorithms tell you how much of each product to ship to which warehouse.

When we made our first FBA shipment, we sent out only one pallet of merchandise. With bated breath, we waited for it to show up in the Amazon back-end as available for fulfillment. Shipping time was about 3 to 4 days from our warehouse to theirs. We got a notification around 9 AM in the morning that our inventory was now available, and by noon, it was gone!

That told us this channel had a lot of room to run, but while we were out of inventory, we were losing sales. But unknown to us, Amazon was 'judging' us. From their perspective, we were not really reliable suppliers, yet. You see, Amazon spends a huge amount of money promoting products, even though many Amazon sellers are also paying Amazon to promote their products.

And because they have built a money generating machine, which, at least partially, includes their warehouse and distribution system, an FBA vendor who can't fulfill is actually costing them money in wasted demand.

Our total replenishment time for this client was about seven days, from creation of the shipment order on our side to arrival of our merchandise at the designated Amazon warehouse. Given the paucity of sales information, yet the clear demand signals, we upped our next order size to 3 pallet loads.

And again, the stock lasted only about one day, before the shelves were cleared. Once again, we saw or rather began to understand better, that Amazon punishes stock-outs[82]. Of course, we were very happy to make those sales, even though the pains of additional cash flow

[82] What you observe is that when you let stock run out, it mysteriously takes far longer for sales to recover when you finally replenish your stocks than it initially took them to sell your stuff.

requirements were quickly bubbling to the top of my problem pile.

We kept upping our shipment volume, until we first filled an entire semi-trailer, then 3, then finally 7 loads. That's when our suppliers, aka, factories, began to buckle under the pressure. We had literally reached the limit of their production capacity, though they were in the process of ramping up capacity.

We also began to experience 'subscription mix' inventory problems. You see, our weight loss plan subscribers received a fairly precise mix of meal replacements and supplements. However, demand for one component of these kits was absolutely taking off on Amazon. So much so, that we were unable to assemble complete kits in our warehouse operation. That's a huge problem when you're selling on subscription.

Our IT System landscape[83] also allowed us to do highly sophisticated Configure, Price and Quote (CPQ) operations. In particular, it allowed us to accept subscriptions that 'renewed' at any time during the month, versus a more typical, and less commercially attractive renewal of 'all at the same time' during the month.

The other thing it allowed us to do was develop and offer customized kits and customized prices, all on the fly, digitally. Customers absolutely loved this. However, it wildly exceeded the merchandise mix capabilities of our

---

[83] www.zuora.com was what we were using at the time. Today, there are many such solutions out there.

homebuilt ERP system.

It wasn't long before we began to experience serious inventory shortages, and customer complaints. The quick fix was to slow down sales on Amazon, but that was leaving money on the table. It also meant Amazon was even more likely, indeed, guaranteed to punish us as unreliable vendors. You won't find this documented anywhere in their help documentation, but I have seen this behavior with multiple Amazon FBA customers of mine.

The more complete fix, of course, involved upgrading the ERP system, finding increased production capacity, and increasing overall productivity across the board. These activities are not exactly within the scope of responsibilities of your typical marketing agency, but I've consistently found that my clients need this level of expertise and thus I can and do offer it, if for no other reason, than it keeps the focus off marketing, which is working, and on to sales and operations, which is not.

Subscription Models Can Be Highly Profitable

What these two case studies reveal is the tremendous opportunity that exist to sell based on a subscription model, regardless of what you sell. To the vendor, a subscription model drastically reduces selling cost on the second and subsequent sales. In fact, it is not unusual for 40% of revenue to come from subscriptions, and more if you get the model right.

That means the profitability of each sales event increases over time. It also means that you have to spend much more of your time ensuring that your customers are happy. No stock outages, no unexpected price increases, no unexpected merchandise mix issues and no quality issues.

It's also why you must know what you're selling. If you truly know what you're selling, then you will be able to explore a subscription model. If you do not, you most likely won't be successful with this approach.

Summary and Lessons Learned

There are many products and services sold as a subscription, even when you don't recognize them as such. The sales model has been around a long time and will continue to be well into the future. To implement a Subscription Model you need to know about and make use of:

- **Razor and Blade Model -** You need to offer a product or service that a consumer is going to consume over and over. Companies have been delivering variations of the razor and blade model since at least the 1800s
- **Explore Innovative Models -** There are many companies offering an ever-wider variety of subscriptions. For example, how about a subscription service model for the plumbing between a customer's water meter and their house and everything inside. It's already being done
- **Make Sure IT Is Up to The Task -** Subscription Sales models impose extreme performance demands on all aspects of your IT systems
- **Be Prepared To Fund More Inventory -** If you sell on Amazon, especially on a FBA basis, and offer a subscription model, for example, diapers, you will need the ability to fund additional, substantial quantities of inventory
- **Chose the Right Subscription Management Models -** Subscription management software models,

especially within the ecommerce space, come in many flavors and with a wide variety of capabilities

- **Get Your Finance System Ready for Subscriptions -** Subscription sales models impose complex requirements on your financial management system. Ensure your subscription management software comes with native integration with whatever financial management software system you use
- **Can You Offer Completely New Combinations with Subscriptions -** A subscription sales model often allows you to offer bundled services to consumers, who would not otherwise buy but a single item from you. For example, a water well driller could combine annual well cleaning to provide an opportunity for customer reengagement that would last a lifetime
- **Learn About Variations To The Model -** A subscription sales model is not always called a subscription model. For example, the US military has been moving toward a "Power-by-Hour" model for their fighter jets and other types of aircraft. This means that instead of buying the jet outright, they instead pay the defense contractor, i.e Boeing or Lockheed, so much per flight hour, even for combat operations
- **Riches in The Niches -** Other interesting subscription models pop-up all the time, if you'll pay attention to them. For instance, did you know you can rent out goats by the day to mow grass?

Many cities are contracting for entire goat herds to perform this service as are many forest management entities around the world. Apparently, the goats work cheap

Turn Commodities into Subscription Model Offers - Finally, many day-to-day consumer products are being repackaged into subscription models by combining some other aspect of the product or service. For instance, you can get bread delivered to your front door on a subscription basis in Spain, where I live

CHAPTER TEN

Package It Right

UPSELLS

If you know your product and your market, you should be able to design a sleek upsell program. What is an upsell? Well, at its most basic level, it simply means seeing if your customer would like to buy something a bit more expensive of the same 'type', which is different from a Cross-Sell, which we will cover in the next chapter.

What are some common and not so common examples? And why examples instead of just explaining the concept? Because it is not always obvious what an upsell is, and I have found that it is best to teach this concept by example.

A common upsell example would be when you are asked if you would like cheese with that hamburger. It is heard millions of times each day. You'll notice the upsell does not usually include the statement, 'at an additional fifty cent cost'. Or whatever number it is. If you dig into this most common of everyday examples, in particular, into the math behind contribution margin, you will understand why this is a big deal.

You don't actually spend much on a slice of cheese, and yet, you can often times add quite a bit to your contribution margin[84]. When you sell billions of anything, that adds up.

Scaling our common examples up a little bit, let's look at buying a car. There are a ton of options you can order on

---

[84] Learn More About Contribution https://www.linkedin.com/learning/running-a-profitable-business-calculating-breakeven/welcome

most cars or could if the manufacturer wanted to offer them. Instead, you are typically offered only bundles (which we will also discuss in the later chapter on bundles) of options. Why?

Again, our old friend contribution margin comes into play here. You see, despite years of retooling factories, it is still no small affair to offer totally unique configurations to a customer segment of one. Apart from the technical challenge of designing and building these highly flexible and by extension, extraordinarily expensive factories, there's the issue of discounts from suppliers.

Suppliers, just like OEMs, are looking to get their production mix right to optimize profit. Unless you have absolutely perfect consumer demand forecasting capabilities, and no one does, you can't walk a product down the learning curve unless you shape demand, which is what is happening when you see those bundles of upgrade options.

Those are all common, if not well understood, examples of upsells. Now let's explore some of the more uncommon ones, which I believe represent where opportunity lies in many markets.

Our first uncommon example, simply because I was surprised it was able to be sold in the traditionally hide-bound B2B space, was a monthly service to validate the information coming out of a clients business warehouse. It was not actually a huge amount of money being charged, compared to the original cost of the datawarehouse implementation. Low 4 figures per month.

However, it had proven to be very attractive to the end user, and thus, customer retention was nearly 100% over one, three and five year periods. It also provided the opportunity for the service provider to consistently 'listen' to the needs of the client and uncover additional service opportunities.

Why is this upsell example considered uncommon? Because in this space, of which this author has over 30 years of experience, rarely is there any post project Go-Live follow up work, unless it's additional project work. There are many reasons for this, much of it coming down to how labor is classified and the need for companies to keep from accidentally turning contractors into employees[85], even at the expense of business performance.

One other interesting upsell model I've run across also combines a subscription model into their upsell model. In this case, one of the big four accountancy firms had redesigned their service offering, aimed squarely at high-net-worth individuals, to be consumable in a more remote, ecommerce fashion.

Prior to this approach, it was widely held that only 'high touch' approaches would work in this lucrative market. However, with careful business process design, and a slow, iterative roll-out, it was found that much of what was being delivered via 'high touch' could just as easily be repackaged into productized services, and thus sold online.

---

[85] This is a situation driven entirely by IRS rules.

It didn't nor will it, eliminate completely, the need for person-to-person contact. But it did drastically improve productivity and increase sales. Of course, the challenge in these types of markets is often the highly intentional efforts of buyers to disrupt the sellers attempt to sell the way they have designed their offering to be sold.

That is why complex sales, which are, by definition, very long sales cycles, can be so very expensive. Clients are ever more demanding, and actually getting through the entire process rarely allows you to position upsells. But it can and should be done. I have often found that when presented correctly, very large amounts of revenue can be tacked onto a contract, if you make it clear why they will need this additional service.

To get more specific, and again, taking an industry I have some experience in, the SAP ERP space, post go-live support is often an area where clients initially want to cut corners[86]. If common sense would indicate that six months or more of support would make sense, it is not unusual to get that chopped down to one month.

The issue usually comes down to lack of clarity as to what support actually means. It also usually comes down to ensuring the client recognizes the risks they are exposing themselves to. This is where it pays to have a well thought out support strategy. It is only by having this documentation ready to present to the client that you can

---

[86] There always exceptions to this rule. Very large companies often set up SAP Centers of Expertise, or CoEs, which come in a variety of configurations, and specifically combine internal and external capabilities, and are a lucrative space for SAP Consultancies to play in.

make them understand that they do not have the resources to take on this task.

In this sort of upsell scenario, one common tactic is to price it in 'chunks'. Meaning break out the implementation from the post Go-Live support pricing. Clients will often want to try to find a lower price for the support part, meaning they will want to get bids on this part separately from your implementation plan.

Clients also know that your support staff will not usually be composed of the same senior level staff involved during the implementation, and therefore, believe they should be able to get a better deal. It's not an incorrect assumption, but it is based on faulty positioning on the part of the vendor.

Why faulty? Because although 100% of the personnel might not be senior level consultants as they were during implementation, at least some of the support team will need to be senior level. This is because even though project documentation can be extremely detailed and complete, it is never fully reflective of the actual project, it simply cannot be. You need some of the implementation team to stick around to perform knowledge transfer.

This process requires time. Introducing this concept early in the sales cycle, primarily through educating the prospect on the complete implementation methodology, will usually 'move the needle' on the need for this type of Post Go-Live support. In fact, it is this education on the complete Customer Engagement Lifecycle or CEL as some vendors call it, that oftentimes seals the deal or even helps in a 'win back' situation.

One such deal I worked using exactly this approach was for a leading airline in Africa. When I was called in, the deal had apparently already been lost to our arch nemesis, whom I will refer to simply as the Red Team, while I worked for the Blue Team. But, if it had truly been 'lost' as in the contract was signed and we are done, no one would usually call me in. You see, within my industry, aviation, specifically, airlines, when I am working with the Blue Team solution, I am usually very confident I can win. Sales guys always are.

In this case, though, we were invited back. To get that invite, we had, as usual, deployed all our tactics to recover or 'win back' a lost deal, including setting up Executive Level sponsorship between the Blue Team "C" suite and the Airline's "C" Suite level of executives, all pilots.

As it happens, not only do I have a 30 year military and civilian aircraft maintenance background, I am also a Pilot and C-130 Flight Engineer. So I speak aircraft maintenance and can identify with the guys on the shop floor as well as with the pilots.

This 'win back' played out as usual, with a call from the Senior Level Account Executive for Travel & Transportation, asking me to accompany her too Ethiopia, where this airline was headquartered. Just to keep my life interesting, we made an intermediate stop in Sudan, where I saw a lot of old Russian airplanes still sitting there from my last adventure in this far flung land.

Upon arrival in Ethiopia, we were met by the representatives of the Systems Integrator we were working with, who showed us their office, and explained how to get on the internet, which was, to say the least, not state of the art. We also checked into what was a newly opened five-star hotel, and the next morning, when we took showers, the shower heads came off in every room.

Despite this inauspicious start, the airline headquarters and maintenance facilities were all first class, being housed in what turned out to be buildings that had been refurbished and were much like U.S. government buildings. They also had, being the first planned operator of the newly released (at the time) Boeing 787 Dreamliner, brand new simulator facilities.

Though the original intent of the trip was, to be frank, somewhat vague, the client still had concerns about awarding the deal to the competitor. Specifically, they weren't really sure the competitor had a real implementation methodology specific to the airline industry. That was my 'hook'.

After meeting with my now very large on-the-ground team (primarily composed of members from our SI partner) I found our ability to hold conference calls severely limited with the 'mother ship' back in Germany due to the poor telecommunications infrastructure. So I decided I would simply 'teach' them the SAP implementation methodology. It was called SAP ASAP at the time. This seemed to be what they were wanting to hear.

As background, I am a Senior Certified SAP Project Manager who also holds a PMP. I have ran and implemented numerous 'Greenfield SAP Implementations' as well as SAP Upgrade Projects, SAP Business Transformation Service Engagements, SAP Value Engineering Engagement and probably most importantly, close to 200 SAP Pre-Sales Demonstrations. In addition, I've often been the speaker on behalf of SAP during numerous marketing events, in the Middle East and Europe.

In short, I know how to listen to an audience and answer their questions and concerns on the fly. When I cannot, I always follow-up when I do get the answer. In this scenario, I found myself with a room full of executives, from all areas of the airline's operations, delivering an impromptu SAP ASAP implementation course[87]. Of course, they weren't going to get a certificate, but they probably could've passed the test when I got done.

This was not the usual course of business for a typical Blue Team engagement. But it proved to be the right course, and ultimately, the course that led to overturning the win against the Red Team, and of shifting this one back to the Blue Team side.

I have to admit, I was quite shocked to actually have this level of executive presence - over a sustained period of time - as I taught them step-by-step how to not just to implement the solution, but most importantly, how to set

---

[87] A full SAP ASAP implementation course, conducted formally, would take about 3 weeks in total. As it was, we spent nearly a full week in what was a mini SAP ASAP course.

up the Post Go-Live support SAP CoE[88] for future success.

Upselling Through Customer Education

That's not only how you sell the initial software solution, it's how you upsell ongoing support operations. For you see, not only do we recommend that large customers set up SAP CoEs[89] to ensure success, but we also have more advanced levels of SAP support available to the enterprise class customers, which this client turned out to be.

There's plenty of 'noise' out in the market about the cost of support[90] being too high, or not delivering as promised. But once you explain why it's needed, why it's insurance against down time and how it is actually highly valuable, and provably so, the sale makes itself.

Sounds easy, right? This is what it takes to know what you sell and make sure you're offering your customers every opportunity to take advantage of everything you actually have to offer. Just about every complex IT system or really, anything slightly complex, usually has an implementation methodology, with many possible options for a customer to choose from.

---

[88] Center of Expertise or CoE. These are internal organizations that are designed to support your SAP system post Go-Live.

[89] SAP CoE or Center of Expertise is an organization established within a client's operation to provide on-going SAP support. There are various types of CoEs as well as various support capabilities.

[90] One of the main selling points of SAP and other COTS (Commercial Off-the-Shelf) software is that you can reduce or eliminate the in-house support staff you have with your legacy systems. When you do a financial comparison of the cost of support being delivered by the COTS vendor vs the cost of your legacy system support staff, then and only then, can you decide whether it is expensive or a better value.

Summary and Lessons Learned

There are almost always opportunities for upsells. There are quite a few 'tricks of the trade' to taking advantage of the upsell opportunities:

- **Design Your Upsell In -** Upsells need to be designed 'in' to your product or service offering
- **Make 'Avoiding a Pain' Your Upsell Strategy -** You need to make it very clear what the baseline product or service is versus the Upsell
- **Make the Pain Visible -** An upsell should relieve the pain the client is likely to feel if they go with only the baseline. First, you must make the pain very visible to the client in terms dollars and cents
- **Can You Leverage a Freemium Model -** The freemium model is a classic version of this approach. You can often do something useful with the free download, but you could do so much more if you upgraded
- **Keep Careful Track of Trade-Offs -** For large complex sales, i.e. SAP and other IT COTS systems, it is almost a guarantee that clients will be limited by budget and tradeoffs will have to be made to win the deal.
- **Keep Your Paperwork Clear -** It is imperative that the trade-off decisions are documented and priced out at the time of contract signing. Otherwise, it is a 100% guarantee that your client will try to expand the scope of what you agreed to. You may know this

phenomenon as 'Scope Creep'

- **Teach to Sell -** Client education about your offering is a proven way to both eliminate scope creep and position eventual upsells.
- **Develop a Clear Upsell Mechanism -** For many lower priced products and services, a 'one click[91]' upsell model can be defined that works very well, if offered correctly.
- **Know Your Source of Profits -** A properly designed and positioned Upsell can drastically increase your Contribution Margin
- **Leave No Opportunity Behind -** There are often multiple Upsell opportunities you can add. The trick is know exactly what you sell.

---

[91] One clear winner in designing 'One Click' upsells with a company called Clickfunnels. www.clickfunnels.com

CROSS-SELLS

Though a Cross-Sell and Upsell look very similar, they are not the same. What's a Cross-Sell? In its simplest form, it means selling something else not directly related to the product or service at hand.

One typical example is socks vs. shoes. If you buy a pair of shoes, you very often also end up buying some socks. Sometimes, the socks go specifically with the shoe, other times, they do not. Perhaps you just bought a pair of dress shoes and decided to pick up some athletic shoes while you were in the store.

But go into any shoe store and look around. What do you see? You see many related products and lots of shoes. The Cross-Sell here is not only socks. It is also shoe cleaning supplies. It is shoe equipment, such as shoehorns, or shoe stretchers to keep them the same size and shape. In fact, if you conduct a search on Amazon, for any single one of these products, you get pages and pages of results.

As it happens, I have some experience in the shoe industry, specifically, the DTC or Direct-to-Consumer market. In this particular business case, it was an athletic shoe brand, specialized in flat bottom shoes for weightlifters. The shoes were worn by celebrities worldwide. We had already found great success with an upsell idea I had, which was to provide individually customizable shoes using Velcro and letters, which was a resounding success.

But then we went looking for cross-sell opportunities.

People don't just wear high-end athletic shoes. They carry them in customized bags, which we added to our product lineup. As the shoe designer was also highly artistic, we branded the print-on-demand shoe bags, to great success.

Then we started studying our customers 'in the wild', and found that, well, they needed coordinated gym bags, that were waterproof and rugged. We added those as well. Soon, we had added just about every conceivable related item a weightlifter or really, any gym rat, might possibly want and added it to our online store.

That's how you make use of expensive, yet plentiful, digital foot traffic to a DTC brand.

This example is fairly simple, just walk into any specialized shoe store, and replicate it. That means it is also not easily defensible from competitors, so you better have a rock-solid product, and be doing on-going customer lead nurturing campaigns[92] to keep them coming back for more.

Let's dive, once again, into Blue Team land and explore Cross-Sell opportunities you may want to design and implement in your own space. One of those Cross-Sell opportunities is training. Specifically, two types of training.

Within the SAP landscape, there are really two types of training:

- Consultant Level Training
- End User Training

---

[92] Lead nurturing refers to the ongoing communication you maintain with a customer, usually via emails and to a lesser extent, SMS messages. It can also include the physical mail, such as sale papers, you send out, as well as coupons and rebates.

End user training is typically delivered during the implementation project. It's part of the methodology. The Cross-Sell opportunity is for the 3rd party software required to design, develop, deliver and warehouse the training. It can be very expensive, and customers need it. It also generates opportunities for training consultants to design and deliver end user training.

Consultant level training is just what it sounds like. It is training designed to create SAP consultants, and comes delivered as Academies, or in single courses. During most implementation projects, client implementation team members will also receive this training, with the goal that by the end of the project, they are trained to the same level as the SAP Consultants.

What may not be so obvious is that there is an inherent conflict between these two types of training that arises on every project. Many clients do not understand the difference between the two types of training. Let me clarify the difference for you so it is clear.

End User training is client specific, while Consultant level training is product specific. By client specific, I mean that it is training customized to show end users, i.e., business process users, exactly how to do their job. Consultant level training, on the other hand, is designed to provide someone the ability to configure and implement a business process and develop the end user training for the newly configured process.

Within complex IT sales, training is one of several examples of important cross-sell opportunities that clients will actually appreciate, if not expect to be offered. It indicates that the vendor is both willing and able to meet all of their needs, even if, for budgetary constraint reasons, they aren't ready to buy everything, all at once.

Summary and Lessons Learned

Cross-Sells represent one of the key areas where you can gain additional revenue. You just have to have thought completely through what you sell. There are a number of lessons you should take away from the cross-selling opportunities discussed here:

- **Many Cross-Sell Opportunities Exist Within Every Opportunity -** For complex sales, there are often numerous cross-sell opportunities
- **Cross-Selling Can Facilitate Budgetary Jiu Jitsu -** In order to meet budgetary constraints required to win a deal, it oftentimes makes sense to put elements of your product or service in the Cross-Sell bucket
- **Leverage Partners -** Many cross-sell opportunities will involve your partners.
- **Make Stuff Available -** Successful cross-selling often means just making sure you have related products readily available in your store, be it physical or online
- **Get Analytical -** Direct-to-Consumer ecommerce platforms, including Amazon, as well as millions of other platforms, have powerful statistical recommendation engines which make cross-selling easier and more profitable
- **Work the Deal From Either End -** Sometimes, the Cross-Sell ends up being the only sell, but can lead back to the primary thing you sell

- **Creativity Is the Secret To Success -** There is plenty of room to get creative with your cross-selling offers.
- **Dig Deep into Your Analytics -** Use your analytical systems to uncover cross-selling opportunities within your customer data
- **Always Talk to Your Customers -** Direct customer interviews, wherein you ask them why they almost didn't buy, will often yield valuable insights about potential cross-selling opportunities
- **Eliminate Inventory Carrying-Cost While Expanding Your Offer -** For ecommerce sites, drop shipping is a key to exploiting cross-selling opportunities.

BUNDLES

Bundling combines the best of Upsells and Cross-Sells into a whole different sales opportunity. How do I define bundling? It is when you combine two or more products, often related, but sometimes not, into a completely new offer. As I have in the past, I will explain this process using some of my own real world business case examples

The most unusual one I have observed was one I was actually involved in during an SAP Business Warehouse Upgrade project. In this case, a US cereal manufacturer was testing a bundle of single serve cereal boxes (1 each) wrapped with a separate product, in this case, a package of cookies, from a recent acquisition.

The part that I found interesting here was that they were using the SAP Supply Chain Management[93] system, known as SAP APO[94], to test this bundled offering out. They had mapped each and every distribution point on all of their delivery routes. This was a national food manufacturer, which sold products in a huge variety of retail distribution points. This included just about every grocery store, and as well, every convenience store, gas station and anywhere else people buy food. In short, millions of retail distribution points.

They were testing hundreds of different elements of the bundle, from packaging, the mix of the product offers, coupons, rebates, availability, and pricing. The business

---

[93] SAP Supply Chain Management is now broadly defined as more than just SAP APO suite. It includes elements from different parts of the SAP System.
[94] SAP APO: Advanced Planner and Optimizer

intelligence system, integrated with both the Supply Chain System and the Customer Relationship Management system, allowed them to do very granular analysis[95] of the results, and make adjustments, at scale.

Of course, testing this sort of bundle at this scale requires a complex IT system landscape, not available too many. That doesn't mean the average retailer cannot pull it off. In fact, one of our Shopify clients, using one of the bundle apps, managed to pull it off with great success. In this case, it was a coffee retailer, who wanted to create virtual bundles of his various coffee sizes, which were being sold via Amazon FBA or Fulfillment by Amazon.

What makes this story relevant and interesting is how this was accomplished using nothing but clever technology. You see, first you have to understand how Amazon FBA works to get the power of this approach. FBA means the vendor has put his stock in Amazon warehouses, in locations defined by Amazon. These warehouses are strategically located around the country to allow Amazon Prime members to be able to place an order and in many cases, get the order the same day, and in a lot of cases, within the hour.

To the vendor (a supplier to Amazon), this translates into having a lot of inventory tied up in Amazon. If you want to offer bundles, as the retailer did in this case, the normal way would be to package your bundles up in your

[95] It must be pointed out that this was challenging from an IT perspective. The actual analysis run was taking up to 4 days to complete on the biggest of big iron, or main frame computers. Even today, this would be beyond the capabilities of many systems.

facility and ship them to Amazon. Your bundle would then have its own SKU or Stock Keeping Unit. This means, in order to add bundles to your offering, you now are tying up even more cash in inventory.

The secret then, is to have software that virtually assembles bundles from your existing individual SKUs. For Amazon, it's all the same on the backend, they will still be executing pick, pack and ship operations on your inventory, but now, 5 or 6 or however many individual items you would have to had bundled together into a new SKU will now be assembled by Amazon on the fly. Now that's a slick use of substituting information for inventory!

Combine Products and Services

There's at least one other flavor of bundling that I think bares mentioning, and that is bundling services and products together. This typically brings together elements of Cross-Selling, Upselling and Bundling into an entirely different class of sales. One example I have seen that works extraordinarily well is in the arena of Engineer-to-Order or ETO manufacturers.

What does ETO mean in practical, real world, if difficult to emulate terms? By way of example, one of my SAP deals, again in the Middle East, this time in Egypt, involved an ETO business specialized in high voltage power lines. They didn't just manufacture the cable, which is, in and of itself, very complex, which most people have no idea about. No, they provided a one-stop shop for the design, manufacture, transport, installation, and maintenance of high voltage power lines.

If you've ever been driving somewhere and saw those gigantic steel towers with electric power lines running between them, stretching for hundreds of miles and sometimes thousands, you've seen this type of product. What does it take to assemble this kind of business? Cash, lots and lots of cash. And engineering talent, manufacturing facilities, transportation experts, finance experts and above all, expert salespeople. Finally, underlying everything, is a complex web of advanced software capabilities, not just SAP, but many other capabilities in the areas of design and engineering.

You see, as you expand the scale of business, the stuff being done gets ever more complicated, with fewer, larger, mega suppliers. The barriers to entry are huge. Yet, there is also an ever-present need on the part of buyers to see a few competitors within their supplier base. This level of vertically integrated delivery capability inevitable creates space for smaller, highly specialized suppliers to play a role.

When it comes to knowing what you sell in the space, what I've found is that the winners never do anything half-assed. That means they have every legal document in place, every type of insurance in place, and every system in place, to compete and win. They also have enough cash to pursue certain deals at risk. Oddly enough, I've also often found myself being asked to help them refine their offer, not just to sell them a system like SAP.

When I have drilled down into their operations, what I usually find is that, if there are issues, such as dealing with sales, it is usually because they lost focus on what their core capability is. Of course, these huge businesses, much like a supertanker, do not easily change directions. You have to give them a nudge long before you ever expect to see a change in direction.

There are many other examples of bundling complex services coupled with custom designed products. For example, within the automotive industry, there is a long-established trend for the OEMs to ask their suppliers to supply ever larger pieces of the product, from Steering Systems that are fully integrated with their onboard radars and lane keeping assist technologies, to complex power trains. That's also why you see fewer bigger suppliers in such supply chains.

Summary and Lessons Learned

Bundling represents a major, often unexploited sales opportunity for many businesses. You just have to have thought completely through what you sell. There are a number of lessons you should take away from the bundling opportunities discussed here:

- **Leverage Technology Effectively -** Whenever possible, look for opportunities to utilize digital technology to create bundles without increasing inventory carrying cost
- **Get Your Customers To Reveal Their Desires -** Use statistical analysis and advanced IT systems to explore what products 'click' with customers
- **Repackage and Repurpose For More Sales -** When dealing with physical products, look for ways to repackage your product into more useful quantities for you customers
- **Use Combinations of Manufacturing Prowess and Service Excellence -** Explore ways to combine your service capabilities with your manufacturing capabilities to bundle more attractive options for your buyers
- **Know Your Financials, Deeply -** Always understand the financial implications of bundled offers on the financials of your offers
- **Flexibility Comes from Knowing Your Numbers -** The more you know your numbers when it comes to Break-Even Analysis and Contribution Margin, the

more flexibility you bring to the market with your bundles

- **Can You Add Even More Value -** Many clients are leaning on suppliers to provide more added-value in the form of coupled design engineering and production engineering.
- **Get Your Mix of Capabilities Right -** Within the realm of complex manufacturing, success depends upon having the right mix of capabilities.
- **Bundling Exist In Most Industries -** There are bundling opportunities in virtually every industry. For instance, would you like to buy a bundled vacation package that includes: Airfare, Hotel and Car Rental?
- **Bundling Saves Your Customer's Most Valuable Asset: Time -** For the consumer, having you bundle your offer oftentimes is saving them time and effort, and they will pay for it. For high end consumers, bundling customization with their purchase is virtually a guaranteed expectation. For an example, go to any high-end mall, such as The Dubai Mall, and you will find luxury goods retailers who successfully bundle high end fashion with many other add-on services. On such interesting one I used was outfitting my apartment. I though it worth mentioning because, in this case, the experience was fairly unique. The store was a high-end furniture retailer, the opposite of the flat pack carriers. I had a newly rented, yet empty apartment, paid for by my

company, and a generous housing allowance, which was par for the course for senior western expats in this region at that time. The way it worked was they assigned me what I think they called a concierge, basically a lady who was both interior decorator and record keeper. She asked me a few questions about what I was looking for, made a visit to my apartment to get dimensions, then we met back up in the store, and did a walk through. She already had pre-picked out much of what she thought I would want and did a pretty good job of it. I had only a few specific requests, i.e., I like big fluffy leather couches and chairs due to arthritis. Going room-by-room, we picked everything out. By everything, I mean everything[96]. They had checklists that kept you from overlooking anything. Magically, everything came in within budget. But that wasn't what made this example worth mentioning to me. What made it worthwhile was, like Santa's Elves, they delivered, assembled and set up everything while I was away doing a deal. You see, they recognized that my most valuable asset was my time, and it was in short supply. Of course, you can get this service most anywhere, but few people actually know about or have the budget to take advantage of it. This store knew about the need and did a booming business. You can too. By the way, when my tour of duty came to an end, they had a market for all of it, which was

[96] You will often hear the term hardbacks and soft packs.

even more exceptional. It took one more monkey off my back.

CHAPTER ELEVEN

New Frontiers

INNOVATIVE SERVICE CONTRACTS

Service contracts have been around a long time. But today, you find them everywhere. The challenge is defining what a service contract is, and then figuring out how you can deliver it at a profit. There are many examples of service contracts, but I want to talk about three specific examples to give you some concrete examples that might inspire you to come up with your own.

The first one comes from my field, aviation. As you may or may not know, maintaining an aircraft is a complex, expensive affair. There are also a wide variety of types of aircraft owners, from the military, which I will address later on, to airlines and to private owners, of both small single engine propeller aircraft all the way up to the Boeing 747, a 4-engine behemoth that revolutionized air travel[97] by bringing long range travel to the masses.

Diving down into the realm of the private jet aircraft owner, specifically, lite jets, is where you see very innovative service contracts. You see, people who own private jets own them because they save them time. They are both status symbol and business tool. What they do not want to do is spend time fixing them because it broke down enroute somewhere along the way.

---

[97] The Boeing 747 was the first successful airliner that could travel transcontinental distances without refueling and make a profit. This ability meant air travel was now open to the masses. While other aircraft could fly across the ocean, their range was limited when compared to the 747, which could fly from New York City to Sydney, Australia, non-stop.

Enter the Service Contract. While it is entirely possible to land at what is called an FBO or Fixed Base of Operations airport and find a mechanic to fix your jet, it is not very convenient for those with the means to own a private jet. Thus, when they buy a jet, they also are usually offered a bundled service contract. These can be very complex, yet, to be commercially attractive, they need to be readily understandable by the client, who often delegates the purchase of such jets to 3rd parties.

These service contracts are innovative in the sense that they provide global coverage, even where the vendor has no physical presence. The complex part of these contracts is forecasting what parts might be needed when, in what quantities and in which locations. Then prepositioning them or otherwise making them available, at geographically key service points around the planet.

In addition to prepositioning parts, aircraft must be highly reliable in the first place. That means that the manufacturer is able to predict failure rates with a high degree of confidence and perform scheduled maintenance before they fail. You can bake all this into the service contract.

There is one final part to being able to confidently offer these types of complex service contracts, and that is efficient billing. Aircraft service events will often generate enormously complex bills, with hundreds or even thousands of individual line items. For the OEM, the challenge then becomes how to settle these invoices across hundreds or even thousands of aircraft. There really is only one viable answer, and that is software, specifically configured for such high-volume service contract settlement actions.

Within aviation, there is another model of service contract that is really a hybrid model of service contract and bundled deal - Power-by-the-Hour or PBH. What is a PBH contract? It means the operator, such as the United States Air Force, only pays for the cost of the flight hour.

How does it work when it is not a PBH sale? Well, traditionally, the USAF bought a jet or really fleets of jets, from the manufacturer, such as the F-16 or F-4. The USAF then had its own maintenance capability. These troops, of which I was one for many years, formed part of a vast logistics infrastructure required to keep the jets flying. The military knew what it cost to fly those jets per hour. For instance, an F-4 might have cost $3,000 dollars an hour to operate considering fuel and maintenance, but not including acquisition cost.

Today, the USAF is asking for an 'all in' cost from the manufacturer, including pro-rata acquisition cost. For example, if you're buying an F-22 Raptor, which may have a price tag of $100,000,000, and perhaps $4000 an hour to fly it, then when you combine those two numbers with a given amount of flight hours, say 10,000, you know what the jet will cost to operate each hour during its operational life.

The challenge is the USAF wants the OEM to actually maintain these jets, even going so far as to put their maintenance personnel into the combat zone, which personally, I don't think is a great idea. But financially, this model makes sense. Politically, though, it's a tough sell.

Those are high-end, not relevant to many, examples. Let's step down to some more mundane industries that are coming up with innovative service contracts: Public Water Utilities and Influencer Marketing Management.

Many if not most people in the United States and many others around the world, get their water via water lines buried alongside the road and elsewhere from Public Water Utility companies. What many people may not realize until they have a problem is that the pipe that runs from their water meter to their house and every piece of plumbing inside their house, is their responsibility. In short, the water company traditionally only ensures you have a water supply to that meter, it's up to you to get it from there to your faucet.

This can and has led to extreme customer dissatisfaction when there are problems with the water lines. That's why several water utility companies are experimenting with offering service contracts that do cover the line from the water to the house and leaks inside the house.

What makes this possible, again, is technology. The water companies cannot and do not keep enough capability in-house to fix these leaky pipes. That's why there are plumbers located throughout the nation. Plumbers, however, are associated with high 'one-time' bills. It's not because they are overcharging, it is because they have a bunch of work to do, it is expensive to do, and not repeat work.

The water company, on the other hand, sells a cheap commodity - water. It has a billing system that is used to send a bill to thousands of customers on a monthly recurring basis. Their new service model is very simple; they sell plumbing service coverage as a business, on a monthly recurring basis, essentially converting the plumbing business into a SaaS type business[98].

The plumber gets steady work, and most importantly, steady cash flow. The utility gets a price break on plumber services due to the volume of business they are sending to the plumber. The consumer sees a small additional charge on their bill and has the assurance that someone will come a running when the pipes burst in the middle of the night when the temperature has dropped to minus 40[99], as it often does in the Midwest.

Influencer marketing[100] is a term you may or may not have heard or even understand if you have heard of it. Many celebrities, both major and minor, engage in influencer marketing. As it happens, I worked for one such person, who was a well-known public figure who also happened to have written diet and exercise books and developed and sold a line of diet products.

As a public persona, he made quite a bit of income from endorsing other's products, and as well, paid many other celebrities to provide product placements in their efforts.

---

[98] SaaS stands for Software as a Service

[99] See winter storm, 1978, Indiana

[100] Influencer marketing is a relatively new term, if not a new concept. What it boils down to is the fact that people look up to, admire and ultimately want to be like famous or influential people.

Because almost everything is digital these days, it's also possible to measure, directly and indirectly almost every mention of any kind on any channel of an influencer.

But monitoring those mentions and fixing false statements is no easy feat. Many businesses have now arisen that offer service contracts, typically bundled with software, to monitor, report on and when needed, attempt to fix 'bad press'. Why would a celebrity care?

In short, money. The current going rate for a product placement is about $5,000 USD per 100,000 followers on Facebook. For a celebrity, this rate goes up, way up, the more followers they have. You ever hear of the Kardashians…

That's why there's a huge and growing opportunity to offer to take on this burdensome task. That price per hundred thousand users rises and falls with reputations. Reputations that have a value all their own.

Summary and Lessons Learned

Innovative Service Contracts represent a major, often unexploited sales opportunity for many businesses and even individuals, such as celebrities. The trick, if there is one, is to identify the pain and quantify the value for relieving the pain. There are a number of lessons you should take away from the innovative service contract opportunities discussed here:

- **Find the Pain, Find the Profit Opportunity -** Offering your customer a service contract helps relieve a pain they don't even know they have
- **Convert One-Time Payments into Recurring Revenue Streams -** Service contracts, when done right, can convert one-time sales in to Monthly Recurring Revenue (MRR) streams
- **Technology is the Great Enabler -** Many service contracts are possible, you just have to have the right technology infrastructure available to execute
- **Complexity Breeds Opportunity -** The more complex the service being offered, the more need for a service contract solution to enable it
- **Your Customers Want You to Help Them Get More from Every Use of Your Product -** Many products exist that can be repackaged into usage based offerings under the auspices of a service contract, not just fighter jets
- **Be Imaginative -** Combining services into new packaged services takes imagination but can pay off

- **Don't Let Billing Technology Limit You -** Billing for complex service contracts is technically challenging and where the secret to success is often found
- **Stratify by Segments -** Service contracts can oftentimes be stratified into different service levels.
- **Extend Your Delivery Capability Using Networks -** You don't actually have to be the entity that delivers the service, use partners.
- **Trust and Accountability Go Hand-in-Hand -** When using partners as part of your innovative service contract offer, having a high degree of trust is of the utmost importance to success. There has to be accountability among all parties

CHAPTER TWELVE

Accept The Challenge

TYING IT ALL TOGETHER

Hopefully, after reading through this book, you've gained a new appreciation for the importance of knowing what you sell. You have come to understand the urgent need for really nailing down this most fundamental aspect of your business.

After struggling for years to hone my offering down to what I thought my customers wanted, it finally dawned on me that though I was offering SAP BW Consulting, and thus the name of my company SAP BW Consulting, Inc., what people kept asking for was help with sales and marketing.

So, I now offer both, because there is a huge market for SAP Consulting, not just SAP BW consulting, but across the entire spectrum of SAP. It would not make commercial sense to abandon that market. However, in the process of learning how to market my SAP BW consulting services, I learned how to help my clients to market and sell their products and services.

For almost all of them, what I found was, to my surprise, was that they seemed to benefit from my 'war stories' when it came to helping them focus on their marketing message. But unless and until I could get them to focus on knowing what they actually sold, success was elusive.

For those who had an 'obvious' product, such as athletic shoes, it turned out to be far less obvious to his actual customers what he was selling than he had assumed. That's why his target buyer persona evolved over time, the data led us to focus on one particular niche aspect of the market, and then to refocus, redesign and repurpose our offer to ultimately, achieve great success.

For those clients who had a far more complex offering, almost always in the professional service space, the challenge has been to get from the traditional consultant 'it depends' to the more client friendly, 'here's the answer'. Though it is true that many consultant's service is an 'it depends' type of offer, it is also true that much can, will and must be productized[101] if the consultant wants to build a successful practice.

When it comes to deciding what to sell, you've seen the importance of conducting market research. I've also shown you how you can conduct much of it, more efficiently than ever before. But nothing beats talking to actual customers to uncover true needs, despite what Henry Ford may have said about faster buggies.

Part of your successful marketing research must include competitor analysis. Unless you're in a unique business offering a totally unique product or service, you've got competitors, direct and indirect, obvious and not so obvious. Within the IT space, your biggest competitor is and will continue to be 'inertia', which means 'do nothing' which is sometimes a safe bet for your customer. You shouldn't be afraid to tell them to do nothing either if you

---

[101] Please refer to Appendix A for an extensive list of productized services for inspiration.

have any integrity.

Part of the reason for conducting market research is to find that elusive need and fill it. It's also why you conduct competitor research, it will often tell you what they think they are selling, and perhaps offer some insight into what you should be offering.

Partnering opportunities often arise from intelligently conducted market research. Sometimes, you find potential partners from your research and can reach out to them and see what partnership opportunity you can make happen. If you're doing Inbound Marketing right, or really, just getting your name out there, potential partners will often find you and reach out.

These partner opportunities can represent potential gold mines of opportunities, or conversely, burn a lot of valuable time. That's why you must be prepared to evaluate each partnering opportunity for strategic relevance to your offering. But in my experience in the SAP Partner space, partnerships offer smaller players a way to play with the big guys while still playing in their niche, whatever it may be.

When conducting marketing studies to determine what you should offer, you've been introduced to the now well established concept of Jobs-to-be-Done. Though an expensive way to figure out what you ought to sell, it nevertheless, offers you the possibility to uncover extremely useful insight into what your customer is actually trying to get done. I think it is probably easier to use in the product world than in the service world, but still offers a useful framework for service providers to leverage when productizing their service.

You've also seen how the B2B and B2C models overlap, and that really, all sales are people-to-people, even when they are machine-to-machine transactions, such as one finds in highly automated automotive factories that rely on Kanban replenishment signals. They all come down to trust. People-to-people trust is established from human interaction, while business-to-business trust uses more formal structures, such as NDA[102]s and contracts. Ultimately, these contractual structures rely on the integrity and honor of each of the parties to the contract to make them work. The enforcement mechanisms available, such as courts, are a last resort and when used, indicate the agreements have not worked nor been honored.

I hope you've understood the importance, when it comes to designing whatever it is you're selling, to understand why businesses buy. I've tried to differentiate why a business buys versus why a consumer buys, though there is a huge amount of overlap in their reasons and motivations.

While it may be popular to say that if you build a better mouse trap, the world will beat a path to your door, that's true only if they have a need to get rid of mice. For others, your product or service had better fulfill one of three

---

[102] NDA or Non-Disclosure Agreement is a type of contract put in place between 2 or more parties obligating the parties to the agreement to refrain from sharing the information about a particular deal, and preventing someone who was brought into a deal from going direct to the customer.

clearly delineated needs:

1. Need
2. Emotional Fulfillment
3. Status Achievement

There may be other reasons but these three, within the context of knowing what you're selling, will set you in good stead. My advice is that if your offering doesn't activate at least one of these emotions, then it probably needs refinement.

No matter what your offering is, it has to be competitive, and that means you have to get your pricing right. Pricing is a complex, challenging subject, for every business. But getting yours right, and out there in the market, is a key to your future success.

I've also shown how the way you package your offering can make all the difference in the world when it comes to your success. Those models include but are not limited to:

- One-Time Purchases
- Repeat Purchases
- Subscription Models
- Upsells
- Cross-Sells
- Bundles
- Service Contracts

There are no doubt other possible ways to package your

offerings, I've chosen to focus on these as I've commonly run across them across a huge swath of customers I've helped over the years. The trick is to remix your offering so that one of these common models applies, test it out, remix it again, and test it out again. Then keep doing that.

CLARIFYING YOUR OFFER

If you've been in business for more than a day, then you will have heard about defining your Unique Selling Proposition or USP. Technically, the concept crosses several if not all boundaries of your business, but I've included it here, in the wrap up to this book, as I think it is critical to understand how it ties back to knowing what you sell.

Importance of Your Unique Selling Proposition

Your USP includes every element of your offer, including not just complete, profound knowledge of what you sell, but also how it is packaged, priced and delivered. It has to be tied back to the 'why' of your customer's reasons for buying. But it also needs to be periodically revisited and refined.

Your USP should be infused throughout the stories you tell your customer's, throughout their customer lifecycle. Keep in mind that what you consider your USP will rarely, if ever, be immediately perceptible or perceived by your customer. It will often take considerable educational efforts to demonstrate your USP to your customer.

That's part of the education and trust building process involved in most every sale, whether long and complex, such as a typical SAP project, or short and direct, such as, for example, the typical car buying experience.

Show The Value

One of your major challenges is demonstrating value. This is often a complex, and therefore, expensive undertaking. The less value you are able to demonstrate, the more likely you are to be forced into the commodity offering box. That may be OK, if your goal is to be perceived as a commodity offering. If that is your goal, then be prepared for 'how low will you go' situations and ever lower margins.

However, if your goal is to make a profit, then you will need to design your offering to create value. If you can't quite put your finger on what value your offer brings, perhaps it is time to revisit your offer.

The Most Powerful Offer

Ideally, you want your offer to press all of the important buttons: Need, Emotional, Status Achievement. Finally, your customers must be aware of and know what value was delivered. These are not just terms that marketing must plant in the conversation, they are elements of perception that your customer must perceive.

CHAPTER THIRTEEN
Wrap Up

SUMMARY

This book is one of a planned nine part series of books. In my original book, "How to Dominate Any Market: Turbocharging Your Digital Marketing and Sales[103]", I identified nine core problems that every customer I have worked with has exhibited:

- Not Sure What You Are Selling Problem
- Growth and Revenue Problem
- Marketing Problem
- Information Explosion Problem
- Sales Team Problem
- The Multi-System Patchwork Mess Problem
- Human Resources Problem
- No Budget Problem
- Lacking the Right Marketing and Sales Platform Problem

Those problems were written about in the order of severity, and thus priority to fix, each business needs to address.

The first, and highest priority problem every business faces is knowing what they sell. Without clarity on this issue, nothing else is likely to work well, if at all. I've tried

---

[103] Lonnie D. Ayers, How to Dominate Any Market: Turbocharging Your Digital Marketing and Sales

to share real world experience I've gained from almost five decades of professional experience, including soon to be 22 years of being an SAP consultant, where I've worked on more than 200 different SAP opportunities in a variety of capacities.

The message from the market that was the genesis for this book was the habit my customers in the Inbound Marketing space developed of asking permission to record our conference calls, which almost always were working sessions for some element of an Inbound Marketing or Inbound Sales project I was working on with them.

These conference calls were far different from the traditional 'seminars' often delivered by companies such as SAP as a form of educational sales content. I know, because in my role as a Senior SAP Industry Principal, for a very long time, I had people on my team deliver them to approximately 2000 people weekly who worked among approximately 59 SAP partners. I am not saying they were not useful or valuable, they were, but I cannot recall anyone ever asking if they could record it, though all were automatically recorded and made available to partners.

I think, upon reflection, the difference between the two approaches was that mine were generally working conference calls, wherein I was actually delivering highly specialized Inbound Marketing service to that particular client. In other words, relevance was high.

What one client in particular said really grabbed my attention. She said "every meeting with you is like attending an entire customized marketing course, with a story blended in to make the point".

Of course, you could take this either positively or negatively, but when I inquired a little further, both she and her boss and the rest of the team chimed in and reassured me that indeed, they were replaying these and learning from them, in fact, they were creating a library, as it was better material than internet marketing guru Frank Kerns[104] delivered, whom I had never heard of before this particular client shared that they were paying a monthly membership fee to him to hear his training and education seminars.

That's what I hope you take away from this book, an ability to take some of my stories and advice and really know what you sell.

---

[104] https://frankkern.com/

CALL TO ACTION

You've read how to identify what you're truly selling. As you can see, it is a little more complicated than find a need and fill it. That's why we offer a complete Sales Audit and Sales Process Design Service. There's no quicker way to find your own product market fit and get your sales process zero'd in.

Book a Meeting with Me using my online meeting system here to get started with your Sales Audit and Sales Process Design Service.

APPENDIX A - PRODUCTIZED SERVICE EXAMPLES

This is a list of companies I found that offer a productized service. Each took a slightly different approach to the task, but I found it useful to study them. I also subscribed or consumed to a fair number of the offerings from the list[105] as well as others.

1. Lead MD, https://www.leadmd.com/best-practices/ Offers a variety of services focused on improving your lead quality.
2. Connex Digital https://connex.digital/, Provides productized SEO audit services
3. Worst of all Design, https://worstofalldesign.com, Offers to help you productize your service
4. Restaurant Engine, https://briancasel.com/ Offers a course on productizing your service.
5. Undullify, https://undullify.com/, Offers small graphic artists jobs as a service
6. Workify, https://www.workify.co, Offers productized White Label Sales services
7. Content Pros, https://contentpros.io/, Offers Content Creation as a service
8. Website Rescue, https://www.ilanadavis.com/website-rescues, Focuses on Shopify Stores

---

[105] These are current as of the time of publication of this book. They can and will change over time.

9. Audio and Video Transcription Services, https://www.rev.com/ Easiest way I've found to get somewhat acceptable first transcript of a video or audio recording.
10. BI Brainz, https://bibrainz.com/, Provides a training course on developing Executive Dashboards.
11. Productize Course, https:/productizeandscale.com/, A productized course on productizing your product or service.

APPENDIX B - SYSTEMS

I've mentioned many software solutions and methodologies throughout this book. This is a list of those solutions and methodologies in case you want to know a little more.

Oracle Designer 2000 Master, A CASE Tool: Computer Aided System Engineering tool, no longer on the market. It was a tool designed to allow you to draw process models, functional models and other elements, press a button, and it would generate both an Oracle Database and the screens and reports to make your system work.

Oracle CDM: The Oracle Custom Development Methodology was available starting in the early 1990s and provided templates and other items necessary to design and deliver a customized Oracle system

SAP ASAP: AcceleratedSAP was the implementation methodology. It is still used to this day on many projects, however, it is now being replaced by SAP Activate.

SAP Activate: SAP Activate is the new implementation methodology of SAP. Conceptually, it means that you select business processes from among a library of business processes and implement them. It goes far beyond that, and still requires highly trained SAP consultants to help you translate your requirements into SAP speak.

SAP Quicksizer©. This is an online tool that is used to initiate the often complex process of hardware sizing and procurement. It uses the concepts of SAPS, a measurement unique to SAP, to determine what size hardware you will need.

SAP: SAP is the name both of a company, SAP and their software. SAP ERP software is the core offering of SAP, the company. However, they actually sell about 1,300 individual software solutions when you take into consideration all of their Industry Specific Solutions, known collectively as IS-Specific Industry Solution, for example, IS-Aerospace & Defense. They also offer a huge variety of software solutions that come from acquisitions that they make on a fairly routine basis. For instance, they bought BusinessObjects and tucked it into their offering.

Zuora: Zuora is a SaaS system designed to facilitate subscriptions. There are now many able competitors. But Zuora is considered enterprise class. It has native integrations with many leading financial platforms. The most important aspect of its functionality is that it allows a salesperson to tailor a deal, online, for a specific customer, and then feedback the parameters of the deal to the financial management and order management system. This can get very complex, and has many implications for the logistics system.

Amazon: Known throughout the world as the 'everything' store, it is the largest online ecommerce platform outside of China.

Google: Most people know Google from using their search engine. However, it is really an advertising platform, and the search engine is just one of numerous businesses that help funnel traffic to its digital properties, so you can run ads on it.

Facebook: A social media platform, used by at least two billion people. It also is an advertising platform, and owns many other properties, such as Instagram. Additionally, it has an ecommerce capability, though very limited.

Index

C

D

E

F

G

H

I

J

K

L

M

N

Q

R

T

X

Y

Z

www.ingramcontent.com/pod-product-compliance
Lightning Source LLC
Chambersburg PA
CBHW030933220326
41521CB00040B/2292

* 9 7 8 1 7 3 6 6 7 6 0 4 2 *